TURNCOAT

An American's 12 Years in Communist China

TURNCOAT

An American's 12 Years in Communist China

The story of
Morris R. Wills
as told to
J. Robert Moskin

Prentice-Hall, Inc. *Englewood Cliffs, N. J.*

CONTENTS

	The Story of Morris R. Wills	1
ONE	Dropout	18
TWO	Battle	25
THREE	Death March	34
FOUR	Decision	48
FIVE	Defection	63
SIX	Self-Criticism	72
SEVEN	Sparrows and Sardines	82
EIGHT	Kai-yen	106
NINE	Disillusion	120
TEN	Police, Places and Pawns	138
ELEVEN	The Return	152
TWELVE	Over My Shoulder	166
	Index	181

The Story of Morris R. Wills

By J. Robert Moskin

The first time I ever saw Morris Wills, he was striding across the covered railroad bridge linking the People's Republic of China to the British Crown Colony of Hong Kong. He wore a green sweater over an open-neck sport shirt and carried a bag in each hand. His wife carried their fifteen-month-old daughter. They were leaving Communist China and returning to the free world.

Wills was one of the twenty-one American soldiers who were captured during the Korean War, survived more than two years in Chinese-run prisoner-of-war camps in North Korea and then chose to go to Communist China rather than come home. They defected.

This book is Wills' story—how he was taken prisoner by the Chinese when he was eighteen, and afterwards spent twelve fascinating and frightening years inside China. He is one of the very few Americans who have gone through Chinese "brainwashing" and surfaced again.

Since Americans have been for so long excluded from China, Wills' story has urgent significance for us. America's involvement in Asia is growing. The Chinese are one quarter of the human race—and now a nuclear power. We need to know all we can about them.

This book is told entirely in Wills' words. His thoughts and reactions stand unlacquered and unretouched. Although I disagree with many of his ideas and conclusions, I have neither censored what he told me nor always been able, of course, to check his accuracy. I am convinced that it is important to hear his dramatic and revealing experiences told in his own way and his own language. His story belongs to the history of our times, and he tells it with considerable, at times surprising, candor.

A word about the title of this book: The twenty-one GI's who went to Communist China at the end of the Korean War have been called many names—traitor, defector, turncoat. Wills says he was not a traitor because he never committed treason or betrayed his country. In his view, he was indoctrinated to be sympathetic towards China and then was given the choice (agreed to by our government and the Chinese) either to be repatriated or not. Today, he does not justify his decision; he is ashamed of it. He says he would not have done it again. He came home disillusioned with the fantasies he had originally been taught about China, and agrees that he can rightly be called a "defector" or "turncoat." He did change his coat.

I first heard of Wills in January 1965 when he wrote from Peking to the East Asian Research Center at Harvard University. He said that he wanted to come home, and, since he knew the Chinese language, he sought a job as a translator at the Center. His inquiry was endorsed by a respected Western newspaperman then in Peking. We at *Look* magazine were told that Wills was planning to come out and that he was one of the most intelligent and stable of the American defectors. The editors decided to investigate whether he had a story that should be told, particularly in view of the war in Vietnam.

At the request of *Look*'s editors, Wills and I communicated repeatedly over the next months through a third party. It was an eerie correspondence. Wills never wrote me directly and I never wrote him—in fact, he didn't know my name. All the mail had to be sneaked in and out of Peking. Even today, I have only partial knowledge of the delicate means that were

2

used. And what we wrote had to be guarded, in case a letter went astray. I did not know whether the Chinese government realized Wills planned to get out, or whether they would permit him and his family to leave. I did not want to jeopardize their escape.

On August 8, Wills wrote our go-between that he and his family hoped to come out in September. He said he could no longer receive or send mail. *Look* photographer James Hansen and I were assigned to go to Hong Kong to meet them and prepare Wills' story. A week later, he surprised us all by writing again, through new channels, saying that their return would be delayed until after October 15. Finally, with the aid of the State Department, especially Asst. Secretary of State James L. Greenfield, and with introductions to Americans who could help us, Jim Hansen and I flew 10,600 miles to meet a man about whom we knew very little.

In Hong Kong we arranged with the British authorities to go to the border when Wills arrived. Fortunately, the American government supported our project, and the British officials with whom we dealt, such as Michael Stevenson and Robert Sun, were knowledgeable and helpful.

Word came out of China that the Willses would emerge on October 19. We arose early that morning and drove northward to the border with a British official, through teeming Kowloon and into the thinly inhabited New Territories. We covered the last miles to China with a police escort.

At a curve in the road, out of sight of the Chinese across the border, we left our cars and walked past the Lowu railroad station to the bridge over the little river separating Hong Kong and China. In the middle of the covered bridge is a narrow strip of sunlight where the two sections of the roof, one part built by the Chinese and the other by the British, don't quite meet—a ribbon of sunlight that divides the world.

A surprising amount of traffic poured across the bridge that morning: Europeans, Middle Easterners, Chinese, entering and leaving China—but no Americans. We weren't allowed in. British officials permitted us to walk as far as the center of the bridge, to that strip of sunlight. Beyond the bridge stood armed Chinese soldiers.

It was a long wait. We learned later that the Chinese were giving Wills and his family a feast, in the hope that they would leave with warm feelings for China. Shortly before noon, they appeared, and Jim Hansen photographed them crossing the bridge and meeting British Senior Immigration Inspector Thomas A. H. Hodson and Miss Nancy Gibson, secretary of the British Red Cross in Hong Kong. As they left the bridge, they were met by U.S. Consul Nicholas Platt, who took Wills alone into a room at the railroad station and asked him a series of questions to determine whether he had violated his citizenship. He had not.

There, at the edge of the free world, I met Morris Wills. It had been a strange sensation, not knowing what kind of man would walk across that bridge. He turned out to be a friendly, thinking person, who knew what he had done and the problems he faced at home.

The next day, after Wills held a press conference at the request of the local reporters, we went to work in my hotel room overlooking Hong Kong harbor, bustling with junks, freighters and U.S. warships. We began recording a total of 45 hours of tape and more than 1,000 pages of transcription. This book is based on those conversations, held both in Hong Kong and New York. On questions relating to Chinese political affairs, I was helped vitally by China expert Donald W. Klein, who was then at Harvard.

Wills interrupted our work to attend long sessions in Hong Kong and Washington with American officials, who wanted to learn as much as possible about developments inside China. I have been told reliably that he supplied our government with a great deal of highly respected information.

This does not make Morris Wills a hero. He doesn't see himself as one. His is a tragic story. He made a terrible decision in Korea—one that, except for his love for his wife and baby,

4

he has lived to regret. It is important to understand how he was brought to make this decision because this same test awaits other young Americans as our country struggles to exist on the same globe with Chinese Communist power. Perhaps reading Wills' story will prepare some future GI in Asia to resist Communist brainwashing.

Why did Wills defect? It would take a skilled psychiatrist to uncover all the reasons. But the reader can see from Wills' own words why he thought he made his decision. He is candid about it.

The reasons start on a hardscrabble farm deep in the Adirondack Mountains of upstate New York where Wills was born and grew up. Those poor, rock-strewn valleys have over the years been the home of stubborn men like John Brown, the abolitionist; Floyd Bennett, the Arctic pilot; Rockwell Kent, the radical artist. Mountain country tends to breed and harbor men who make up their own minds out of their own experience.

A big farm boy, rather brighter than average, Wills liked to hunt and fish and tinker with cars. His mother died when he was twelve. He dropped out of high school and enlisted in the Army when he was seventeen. In Korea, Pfc. Wills fought and killed Chinese and was severely wounded in combat. Two weeks after his eighteenth birthday, he was captured by the Chinese in a night battle. Then followed a brutal, degrading "death march" northward to the prison camp near the Yalu River, on the very border of China. On the march, many men died and, Wills tells us, the struggle to live crushed most of the survivors' moral standards and broke their spirit.

During two years in the POW camp, Wills' bitterness grew. The fear of being left there to rot, the despair of ever getting out, the lack of preparation to meet Communist indoctrination—all left a vacuum that the Communists filled. Wills was conditioned to respond to reward and deprivation and, in the end, was persuaded that Chinese Communism is a noble experiment and the United States an exploitative

5

society. The Chinese indoctrination took. Wills wavered until the last moment and then chose to go to China.

Under Operation Big Switch, the twenty-one American GI prisoners—and a British Marine who went with them—spent three months in a "neutral zone" supervised by Indian troops. There, American "explainers" were supposed to prevail on the GI's to return home. Of the Communists' 359 prisoners of all nationalities who chose not to be repatriated, 250 attended such explaining sessions. The Communists convinced the twenty-one Americans and the British Marine not to listen, and they never did.

If Chinese indoctrination had been less successful and if Chinese control over the Americans in the neutral zone had been eliminated, as it was supposed to be, Wills and the others might have changed their minds. They would have heard Joseph D. Lohman, now dean of the School of Criminology at the University of California, make a long statement that began: "The United Nations and the United States are thoroughly committed to the principle of individual freedom of choice in regard to the question of repatriation. Indeed, the U.S. persisted through the Armistice negotiations in guaranteeing the right of the individual prisoner of war to himself decide whether he desired to be repatriated to his native land or to establish his residence in a neutral country. The U.N. and the United States continue to subscribe to this great principle."

Lohman's statement warned the young men: "If you should decide not to return to the U.S., you will have made a most fateful decision, one which would change seriously the whole course of your life. . . ." He appealed to them: "Whatever your experiences may have been, your government desires to discharge its responsibility to you, your parents, your neighbors, and your fellow Americans by making certain that your final decision is the one you really desire, that it is without duress or coercion and that you, with full information and an open mind, see your decision as the preferable one, the one best for you, for your loved ones, for your future, and for all that you hold dear."

And a final warning: "Now is the time to seriously consider that there is nothing more humiliating than to discover that one has been a tool, used for someone's questionable purposes and then later tossed aside like an old shoe. Be certain in your own mind that you are not just grist for the propaganda mill. Here and now you can thoughtfully determine how much of the future charted for you in a strange land is a fairy tale that will fade with the years."

After he had gone to China, Wills may have wished he had heard and heeded those words.

On January 23, 1954, even before they entered China, all twenty-one were dishonorably discharged by the Secretary of the Army with the concurrence of the Secretary of Defense. The discharges were effected by administrative order, not by court-martial. The Army accused twelve of the twenty-one of informing on their fellow POW's; Wills was not among them.

The twenty-one had joined the Army from sixteen states. Most of them had grown up in broken homes and under difficult conditions and had not completed high school. Three had served in World War II. Only one member of the group had been drafted; all the rest had enlisted.

In addition to the twenty-one, two GI's, while still in the neutral zone, had reversed their decision to go to China and elected to go home. They were taken into custody by the U.S. Army and charged with collaborating with the enemy. One was sentenced to ten years in prison; the other to life imprisonment, later cut to twenty years. Both were released by 1959, but the effect of these sentences on the ex-GI's who had gone to China can easily be imagined.

The first defectors to return home from China in July 1955 were also seized by the military police. But the United States Supreme Court ruled that the Army had no jurisdiction over former servicemen for crimes committed while they had been in uniform, and they were released in November. They were never brought before a civilian court and they received back pay for the period they served as POW's, up until the time they had decided to go to China. Two others who left, later applied for back pay and were told the statute of limitations for such claims had run out. Some military officers regretted the haste with which Secretary of Defense Charles E. Wilson had ordered the twenty-one dishonorably discharged.

As Wills describes so graphically in this book, Chinese Communist "thought reform" or "brainwashing" played a central role in his decision to refuse repatriation—and then later to stay in China. He and his fellow defectors learned to do the Chinese' bidding with conviction. The Korean War put "brainwashing" in the American vocabulary. The process is often misunderstood. It was used in the Soviet purges of the 1930's and it is said that the Czarist police developed it even before the Bolsheviks. Sometimes physical coercion and brutality have been applied, but the Chinese more often rely on subtle and insistent persuasion. With the American prisoners of war, they mixed physical deprivation with fear of death and torture. Standards of morality and self-pride were broken down; authority among the prisoners was destroyed. Finally, when there seemed no hope of an end to the enemy's control, the indoctrination began.

Why did Wills crack under these pressures when so many other GI's endured them? In Korea, 7,190 Americans were captured by the enemy. There were many cruel "death marches"; on one, 500 of 700 POW's perished before reaching prison camp. An estimated 2,730 Americans died in the camps.

Most GI's who survived the death marches and the lonely, hopeless imprisonment did not defect. Certainly, other POW's were politically naïve. Others had mothers who died when they were young. Others resented the Army and were embittered by their long captivity. But most of them overcame

8

the brainwashing. Wills failed to. He failed to detect the distinction between fact and fiction. At the end, he chose fantasy. There is no desire in this book to excuse what Wills did; only an effort to understand him.

After the war, a special committee, The Secretary of Defense's Advisory Committee on Prisoners of War, was appointed to study how American servicemen had reacted to Chinese imprisonment and thought reform. On July 29, 1955, the committee issued a lengthy report to the Secretary of Defense, stressing that the American POW's had been inadequately prepared to meet enemy propaganda, interrogation, indoctrination and coercion.

"The committee heard a number of ex-P.O.W.'s who stated that a knowledge of communism would have enabled them to expose its fallacies to their camp-mates," the report said. "While it might be argued that few of the men became sincere converts to communism—indeed, the percentage seems to have been infinitesimal—the inability of many to speak up for democracy distressed loyal P.O.W.'s. Active collaborators aside, there were other passive prisoners that 'went along.' They lacked sufficient patriotism because of their limited knowledge of American democracy. It seemed that these P.O.W.'s in question had lost their battle before they entered the service. . . ." Wills was one of those unable to withstand the Communists.

The committee also raised an almost unanswerable question: "Perhaps the Red enemy worked harder on the Americans than he did on the other prisoners. An American who signed a propaganda leaflet, a peace petition, or a germ warfare confession, was a big feather in the enemy's hat. Many Americans in Communist P.O.W. camps signed something or wrote something. Out of 78 men under various forms of duress, 38 signed germ warfare confesssions. Forty did not. Both groups were under coercion. Why did some men break, and some refuse to bend?"

The committee told the Secretary of Defense that the steps

9

the armed forces had taken to meet the strains of enemy interrogation "had been decidedly inadequate." As a result, the Department of Defense revised its Code of Conduct and established a new training program. The effectiveness of this program cannot be judged until we learn what has happened to the American POW's in Vietnam, a number of whom have already made statements and written public letters condemning their country.

After his two years as a prisoner, Wills lived for twelve years in Communist China. He witnessed China's struggle to climb out of poverty by marshaling her 750 million people—her greatest resource and greatest burden—into blue-clad armies of workers. He traveled over much of the country and had long and often intimate contact with Communist Party cadres (bureaucrats), students and members of foreign embassies in Peking. He could communicate with the Chinese in their language and he came to understand them. First he reacted with soaring hope; slowly it changed to disillusionment and despair. What Wills tells us about his life in China is not only a compelling personal story but unique and important.

Inside China, he and the other defectors had to submit to the terrifying process of "self-criticism" that kept the Chinese Communist society glued together. In small study groups, they repeatedly had to attack each other and confess their "sins" to their fellows and the omnipresent Party. Drained of self-dignity, they were made to feel evil and worthless. And when each man had purged himself, Wills reports, he experienced a euphoria of religious fervor and the excitement of joining a crusade and sharing a powerful ideology. Shame was replaced with conviction.

Wills lived through the hardships and the repressions as the Communist rulers tried to consolidate the nation, build the economy and contain the hostile forces they envisioned surrounding China. When he arrived in Korea in January 1951, the Chinese Communist regime, inaugurated in Peking on October 1, 1949, had been established for only fifteen months, and when he rode across the Yalu River into China in February 1954, the young government was still battling enormous problems. The leaders had begun the process of industrialization and had fundamentally changed the nation's social structure.

They tackled a quick succession of foreign problems. By October 1950, barely a year after gaining power, they plunged into the Korean War to preserve the North Korean buffer state. They drove the United Nations' forces back below the 38th Parallel and fought in Korea until 1953, when Stalin's death apparently made negotiations possible. In Indo-China, they helped their allies defeat the French in 1954. They mobilized against the Chinese Nationalists, dug in across the Taiwan Strait. After 1959 they fought India over thousands of square miles of disputed territory. They were dogmatically determined to kick all "imperialists" out of Asia—a goal on which they are still bent.

Without the Chinese Communists' successes, America's entire course in Asia—including two bloody and costly wars to date—would have been different. The Communists made China a nation we cannot ignore. And they attacked the United States' post-World War II involvement in Asia: its presence in South Korea, its occupation of and then its alliance with Japan, its close ties with the Philippines, its support of the Nationalists on Taiwan, its formation of the Southeast Asia Treaty Organization, and, in more recent years, its military support of South Vietnam. As the United States became the strongest power in the Pacific and pushed the western frontier of its might against the shores of East Asia, the Chinese leaders taught their people that the United States is an "imperialist aggressor" and "Enemy No. 1." They demanded that the United States get out of Asia and leave the smaller noncommunist nations, which the United States was committed to defend, to Chinese domination.

During Wills' years in China, her rulers wrestled with the Soviet Union for leadership of the Communist world. Wills arrived in China as Nikita Khrushchev was coming to power in Moscow. From the Soviet Union's 1952 proclamation of "peaceful competition" with the noncommunist nations through the Bandung Conference in April 1955, the Chinese made some effort to coexist. But as Maoism became China's ultimate doctrine for Asia, they challenged the Soviet Union's superiority in the Communist world. From their own history and from Japan's initial defeat of the European colonial powers in World War II, the Chinese Communists took the lesson that war leads to the death of "imperialism." In contrast, the Soviet Union understood the nuclear dangers in today's world. Increasingly, it was becoming a "have" nation interested in less belligerent relations with the United States and the instigation of local Communist movements without war.

After the split opened between the Soviets and the Chinese Communists, the Soviets denied help to China in the 1958 Taiwan Strait crisis, refused in 1959 to share their atomic arsenal with China and withdrew their vast technical assistance in the summer of 1960. The Chinese leadership reacted by attempting instant-modernization. With their population growing by more than twelve million a year, radical measures seemed called for if progress were to be achieved without outside help.

The Chinese leaders tried fanatically to push China into full-scale communism and attempted to substitute manpower for absent capital. Their Great Leap Forward in 1958 was a mass effort to stimulate industrial production and form agricultural communes to increase food production. This short-lived, convulsive effort made some advances at tremendous costs in wasted effort and peasant exhaustion and unrest. Even today, China has not solved the problem of feeding its rapidly increasing population. In *Twentieth-Century China*, O. Edmund Clubb quotes Michael Borodin, whom the Soviets sent to China in the 1920's, as saying, "The only Communism possible in China today is the Communism of poverty, a lot of people eating rice with chopsticks out of an almost empty bowl." And the threat of hunger remains.

Rationing went into effect as early as 1955 and by the summer of 1959 there was widespread hunger. Wills shared this tragic period, though as a foreigner he was protected against severe shortages of food. Production continued to drop, and by 1961 China was buying grain from the free world. China's traditional sense of superiority has been frustrated, so far, by hunger. It is hard for a nation both to carry a begging bowl and be arrogant—but it is not impossible.

China's domestic failures, her receding influence in the underdeveloped world and her internal struggles over economic solutions and power all created opposition to Mao Tsetung's ideological and political domination. And in February 1956 the Soviet Union's dramatic rejection of "the cult of the personality" undermined Maoism and apparently made Wills think afresh about what the Chinese Maoists had been teaching him.

Wills' disillusionment paralleled these shock waves preceding Mao's counterattack—the Cultural Revolution. This upheaval officially began within weeks of Wills' leaving China; he witnessed its beginnings. One of the astounding facts about this momentous and chaotic outburst was Mao's use of force—first students organized as Red Guards and then the army itself —to oppose the apparatus of the very Party he headed. He was determined to make sure that the Chinese Communist Revolution marched forward, to enforce obedience to the Party and to indoctrinate the young to treasure the revolution. He sought to convert his ideas into the dogma of a new, secular Chinese religion—"the thought of Mao Tse-tung."

Under the chaos and harsh realities of life in China, the effects of Communist brainwashing wore off. Most of the American defectors found the regimentation, the conformity and the puritanism unbearable. The Communists sought to destroy personal relationships, even family loyalties, in the

13

service of the state. They wiped out any right of privacy. The state dominated the individual. Wills experienced this molding of the "mass mind," the growing suspicion of anyone not Chinese, and the demand that men and women live out their lives as cogs in a cruel effort to overcome an ageless, mountainous poverty. His enthusiasm was crushed.

One of the major reasons that Wills stayed in China longer than most of the group was that, as a foreign student at Peking University, he had relative comforts, a special status and some freedoms. He was released from thought-reform discipline and free to think for himself.

Slowly, he saw that the Communist system had too many faults to tolerate. He came to expect a head-on confrontation between China and the United States, and did not want to be trapped in China. He felt increasingly alienated from the Communist society, simply because he was not Chinese and because, in his stubborn way, he would not stick completely to the doctrinal line. Above all, he was shocked by the Communists' brutal punishment of the girl who dared to love him.

When Wills finally left China, he had much better luck than most of the others who had come out. Of the twenty-one, eleven had fled by the end of 1958—after less than five years there. One had died in China in 1954. By the time Wills went, only three were known to be still there: Clarence Adams from Tennessee, who has since come home; Howard Adams, a World War II Bronze Star holder from Texas, and James Veneris from Pennsylvania, also a World War II veteran and the oldest of the American defectors. Three others had gone to Europe, one to Czechoslovakia and one to Poland, the home countries of the girls they had married in China, and the third to Belgium, where he had been born. The British Marine had also gone home.

Most of the fifteen who have returned to the United States have had a difficult time. A recent check found only five known to be employed. Several have been arrested; at least three have spent time in mental hospitals.

Wills fared better than most for several reasons. He was the youngest of the group, excepting only Richard Tenneson, who is a few weeks younger and who had left China in 1955. Moreover, Wills is quiet and cautious, and acts with considerable self-control and self-awareness; he thinks out his moves carefully.

He planned ahead. He decided his greatest asset would be his knowledge of the Chinese language. With the support of others, particularly Charles Taylor, the Toronto *Globe and Mail* correspondent in China, he sought employment before leaving Peking. Harvard University, the University of California and Columbia University all expressed interest in his abilities.

Once in the United States, Wills found a job at Harvard's East Asian Research Center as a research associate and librarian. Harvard is now planning to publish a monograph by Wills on Peking University, part of a study on Chinese higher education. As a result of his work at Harvard, he was recommended for and won a fellowship in the Foreign Area Fellowship Program of the American Council of Societies and the Social Science Research Council. Under this program, he began studying at Columbia to become a professional librarian working with Chinese research materials.

For the most part, Americans seemed to accept Wills without resentment. Perhaps in judging him, they wondered about their own threshold of pain and agony and how much brutalizing they would have been able to withstand.

When Wills took his wife and baby home to West Fort Ann, New York, he seemed to walk on tiptoes. "I haven't really had a home in fifteen years," he told me. His mother still rests in Brown's Cemetery, but much had changed in those fifteen years. One sister, who was eleven when he left, is now a mother. Skipper, whom he had raised from a pup, is dead.

15

The family welcomed him warmly, especially his aunt, Mrs. Dorothy Andrews, who had written to him regularly in China. Jimmy Winchell, his boyhood friend with whom he had joined the Army and gone all the way to Korea, was glad to see him. And Wills' father greeted him with love, saying simply, "I never thought I'd live to see my boy again. Now I'm ready to die."

The importance of what Wills has to tell us is attested to by the attention that the relatively brief *Look* article received. The AP and UPI, newspapers from coast to coast and publications of the military services carried stories. The Voice of America beamed an interview with Wills to Asia. From Peking came reactions of distress about many of Wills' revelations.

Schools across the country used the article in their teaching programs about China and communism. The U.S. Army Adjutant General School at Fort Benjamin Harrison, Indiana, made it "must" reading in its Personnel Management Officer Course. General Matthew B. Ridgway, who had succeeded General MacArthur in command of the United Nations forces in Korea, wrote to *Look*'s editor William B. Arthur about the article: "Its publication should straighten out some distorted thinking on Communist China and by doing so perform a public service."

From Harvard's East Asian Research Center, Associate Director John M. H. Lindbeck wrote: "To me one of the most illuminating features of his account is the sense one gains of some of the struggles and feelings of his Chinese and foreign Communist friends. They come through as human beings who also react against the degrading arrogance, deceit and callousness of China's Communist power elite. Perhaps this is our chief hope for a change in China.

"I certainly agree with you that Wills' experience can serve a very useful purpose for other Americans who may fall into the hands of the Chinese."

This is the significant point.

Why read the story of a turncoat? The Korean War and

the more recent war in Vietnam teach us that Americans must be prepared, as best they can, to endure the almost unendurable privation, degradation and brutality that often are the fate of prisoners in Asian warfare. And those who survive these agonies must be ready to meet the increasingly perfected techniques of indoctrination and brainwashing.

More than twenty American servicemen have written public anti-American statements from their prison camps in North Vietnam. Perhaps this book will help some future young men to triumph over such hardships and manipulation. If it saves even one, this effort will have been worthwhile.

I

DROPOUT

On February 24, 1954, I turned my back on my country and my family, and entered Communist China. I wanted to live there and help the Communist Revolution. I had been convinced that communism was the answer to everyone's problems.

I had been taken prisoner by the Chinese in the Korean War two weeks after my eighteenth birthday. After two endless years in a Chinese-run POW camp in North Korea, up near the Yalu River, I went willingly with twenty other American GI's into China. Today, I am ashamed of that decision, but I will not deny that I made it voluntarily—and enthusiastically.

I am home again now—an American citizen with a wife and a baby daughter—and I know that the great struggle between China and the United States has only begun. It will go on until either we Americans are out of Asia or until the Chinese are defeated. Before it is over, many young Americans will face experiences like mine. I knew, when I read about Americans captured by the enemy in Vietnam, that they could not imagine the ordeal ahead of them. Perhaps my story will help some of those who may yet be captured.

Let me clear up one point right here: we Americans toss around the word "brainwashed" without much idea of what it means. Brainwashing is not done with electrodes stuck to your head; you are not turned into a robot obeying the orders of a Chinese master. What we call "brainwashing" is a long, horrible process by which a man slowly—step by step, idea by idea—becomes totally convinced, as I was, that the Chinese Communists have unlocked the secret to man's happiness and that the United States is run by rich bankers, McCarthy types and "imperialist aggressors."

Before I was taken prisoner, I knew nothing about Karl Marx or about communism. I was born and grew up on a farm in the Adirondack Mountains in upstate New York. Our place was a mile out of West Fort Ann, which is only a country store and a white Methodist church, where we went to church occasionally. When I was in China, I found an old *National Geographic* magazine that had some pictures of my area. It said the British once had a post at Fort Ann.

My ancestors came to America as far back as 1640 and fought in every war in American history, just as I fought with the U.S. Second Division in Korea. We are proud of our family's story and we have a family tree at home that shows what many of our people did. My father's people were originally Welsh; my mother's, the Coplands, were Dutch. One ancestor in the American Revolution was wounded defending New London, Connecticut, when Benedict Arnold attacked it in 1781. One was the chief marshal in the parade at the laying of the cornerstone of the Bunker Hill monument. Another was seized by the British in the War of 1812, escaped and enlisted in the U.S. Army. Some of us were pioneers in Ohio, Indiana and Iowa, and in the Civil War one was the last survivor of his company in the 27th Iowa Volunteer Infantry. My father served with the artillery in World War I, and five of my uncles fought in World War II, two as Marines. They were my boyhood idols.

Our roots in America go very deep; our love for this country is very strong. What I did at the end of the Korean War, I did despite these roots and this love.

I was born on May 3, 1933, in the same house my father still lives in, and the first thing I can remember was when I was about two years old, I was playing outside in my cart, and the handle struck me and broke an abscess in my appendix. My father rushed me to the hospital in Glens Falls in his car, and I reached there just in time. I can remember that and lying in bed next to a boy who had both his legs hung up in casts.

I was just sort of an average boy, except that I had asthma and was sickly and thin and it was extra hard for me to walk to school in the winter. There was a little white, one-room schoolhouse about a mile away and the winters got terribly cold and sometimes we had to wade through snow two feet high or more to get there. I was out of school most of that first winter, but I can remember struggling back and forth to school in this snow. Lots of the time I would have to lie down at home and just wheeze away. I was absent so much that I failed the first grade, but by the next year they had built a large, red-brick central school in Fort Ann and started a bus, and I did the first year over.

Because I had been sickly, my mother was always rather especially fond of me and protected me more than my brother and four sisters. Some of my earliest memories are of my mother. I remember she had very long, black hair. She liked to drink tea every afternoon, right after lunch. And she had a canary that no one else could touch; only she could feed it. Right after lunch she would feed her canary, and then she'd have me comb her hair, run a comb through her long black hair while she drank her black tea, there, for a few minutes. That's one of the first memories I have. I'd comb her hair and she'd drink her tea. Sort of quiet and right after lunch sort of peaceful.

My mother died when I was twelve. She had a bone tumor on her knee and lived in great pain the last six months. Finally, they had to amputate, but it was already too late. Even so, she might have pulled through, but she had yellow jaundice and died in the Glens Falls hospital. She's buried in Brown's Cemetery just down the road from our farm, and when I go there and stand among those old stones, I have the feeling of returning to the place of my ancestors. This is where I was born and grew up and where all my friends had been born and brought up. It has always been home.

My father worked hard and was always tired and read his paper, listened to the news and went to bed. On Sundays, whenever he could, he used to take us out on a picnic with hot dogs and soda pop and we would pick berries. He was never much involved with us kids, but after my mother died, he certainly tried. My mother was strictly against anybody smoking or drinking, but my father didn't care. He believed if you are going to do it, do it in the house in front of us, not behind our backs.

That same year after my mother died, I started working after school on my uncle's farm up the road, my father's sister's place, helping him in the morning and evening to feed the cows and run the milking machines. He had thirty to forty head. His hired man had quit suddenly and he couldn't do all the chores himself. Eventually, I began living there and going home on weekends.

On our farm, we had cows too, and my brother and an uncle, Joe Andrews, did the farming. My father worked on the roads for the county. He ran all sorts of machinery—graders, bulldozers, shovels—and during summer vacations, when I was young, he'd take me with him and let me operate the machines. I got so good that he'd get off and I'd do it. That was the best part. I loved machines, any sort, and I'm good with machines.

In school, I did about average. I could stay up with the rest without working. The teacher I remember best was the "ag" teacher, Mr. Penfound. He was very good with the boys; he let you swear as long as you weren't too vulgar and smoke if you were moderate about it. He used to organize trips to auctions and cattle shows. I liked him best. And I remember Miss Gilmore in the sixth grade. She was the sister of the uncle I worked for and lived with. She was probably the strictest teacher there. Everyone was fearful of her. I was never disciplined by her because I knew how strict she was, and always toed the line. But I remember her beating a friend of mine over the head with a newspaper one day. Actually, she was fair. There was one teacher I didn't like: a big teacher who was always trying to pit one of us against another. He'd like to see us beat each other to pieces. To keep us under control, he would use one against the other; divide and rule.

I suppose more than half my free time I spent fishing or hunting. There were streams and ponds all around there. I still remember my first trout—a huge one; it weighed about three pounds. I caught it just below our house. Caught it illegally, really. One of my uncles taught me to snare trout. You rig up a pole and line and make a snare out of very fine copper wire. When you see your fish, you drop this in the water and work the noose right behind his gills, without touching him and without him seeing it. You have to be very cautious. Then the wire would catch him and you have to snatch it up quickly.

Later on, I bought myself first a shotgun and then a rifle. No one taught me to shoot. I shot left-handed, so later in the Army I had to learn all over again. I used to hunt all the time —mainly squirrel, rabbits, partridges. I'd go deer hunting occasionally, but I think I only shot two, the second when I was home on furlough. You aren't supposed to hunt at night with lights, but it was common then in upstate New York. When I was home on furlough, a friend and I were going along the road very slowly, looking under apple trees, because deer like to come down and eat fallen apples. We came on a small herd of four or five, and I shot one.

All my friends went hunting and fishing together. The first buddy I ever had was Alfred Chase. We'd always been together. He was a year older, and when I was still sixteen, he joined the paratroopers, and while I was in Korea, he was in the 82nd Airborne at Fort Bragg and came home one Sunday with a friend's car. He was late in leaving, and driving back to camp he had an accident and was killed.

When I was fifteen, I bought my own car and just drove it

around. I'd been driving since I was twelve; all the kids in the country do—trucks, tractors and everything like that. Later, I bought a '37 Ford, but I still didn't have a driver's license. Still too young.

Alfred Chase and Jimmy Winchell and Sonny Graves and I would go out together. We took turns with our cars. We had some girls we would date in Glens Falls and Hudson Falls; no one had a steady girl. Or we would date girls from our school, take them to a movie and to a little place we called Louie's in Glens Falls for hot dogs. Some nights we would go to Glens Falls and play pool; we'd play rotation, loser pays. Once in a while, when we wanted to show off, we'd buy some beer; rarely whiskey—it was expensive and no one really liked it. We would just drink it to pretend we were grown-up. Jimmy later married one of the girls we dated, and Sonny married one of the girls from our school.

As I grew older, I wanted more and more to get out of there, to get away from the farm. In the spring of 1950, when I was sixteen and a junior in high school, a classmate, "Junior" Reynolds, and I decided to drive to New York City. We got as far as Ravena, just below Albany, and got stopped by the cops. Of course, I didn't have a driver's license and at first neither of us would tell the cops where we came from. They kept us in the county jail over night and, after we told them, they called our fathers. My father came down and picked us up. That's the farthest I ever got from home.

Now I was determined more than ever to get out. I dropped out of school. I wanted to join the Air Force and travel. I didn't see any future in farming. Jimmy Winchell and I decided to join together, but he couldn't get in the Air Force because of his teeth. We wanted to stick together, so I said, all right then, I'll join the Army with you. My father didn't like the idea; I was barely seventeen and still growing. I was five foot ten then; now I'm six foot two and a half. But I was determined. I was going one way or the other. So he signed the papers reluctantly.

The Korean War had just started and they were desperate for men. I had high blood pressure, but the medical examiner in Albany asked me if I had been drinking the night before. I figured something was wrong. I hadn't been drinking but I said I had. He passed me, and on July 27, 1950, I was sworn into the Army.

II

BATTLE

Funny thing, as soon as I left home and got to Fort Dix in New Jersey, I didn't have asthma anymore. Jimmy and I had our basic training together there and armored training at Fort Knox, Kentucky. In November, we came home by Greyhound on a furlough. I spent most of the time hunting. We were going to Korea, although they hadn't told us that. They just told us to report to Chicago. I more or less guessed we were going to Korea, but at that time Korea was just some remote place; I didn't have the faintest idea where it was.

The night our furlough was up, my father drove us down to the train in Albany. He shook hands and said, "Now I want you to be careful and come back." And I said, "Don't worry; I'll be back." I didn't say anything about being careful; I said I'd be back. Then I turned and got on the train. That was the last I saw of him.

Jimmy and I got all the way to Korea together in January 1951. This was about two months after the Chinese Communists had entered the war. We went to the 38th Regiment of the Second Division as replacements. I was put in E Company and he went to F Company. Jimmy was a runner, and occasionally I'd be out on some hill and he would be going through and would stop and see me. One night we were holding a road, and the regiment was having a ferocious fight up in the mountains. The hill changed hands about four times that night. Next morning I heard from a friend in F Company that Jimmy had been wounded, legs all shot up, wounded in a half-dozen places. He had gotten hit in the first attack and had been left in a foxhole. The Chinese had taken him three times. He had been retaken each time and the Americans carried him out of there that morning more dead than alive. I thought he probably would die but I heard later that he had lived. When I finally got home after my years in China, he told me that he had taken a machine-gun burst, and before he was through, he had to have twenty-six operations.

On the ship from Japan to Korea, I did something I have regretted all the rest of my life. We were issued C rations. Well, I'd never liked lima beans, and C rations often had a can of lima beans and ham in them. I opened my C rations and there was a can of these damned lima beans. I tried to give them away, but nobody would take them. When we got to Pusan harbor on January 16, we were ordered not to leave anything on the ship. I had to do something with the lima beans, so I threw them out the porthole. I've never regretted anything more in my life. While I was a prisoner starving in North Korea, that's all I could think of: that can of lima beans, lying on the bottom of Pusan harbor. That thought stuck with me throughout my time in prison. I was starving and I had thrown away a can of lima beans. Every time I would think of food, I would think of lima beans. I'd wasted it when people were starving. Now I was being punished.

After riding in a truck all day, we pulled into the 38th Regiment headquarters at midnight. The next morning I was put in the machine-gun squad of the first platoon of E company. I was an ammo carrier with an M-1 to give protection to the machine gun. Later on, we lost the machine gunner, and I got to be assistant machine gunner. Before I was captured, I was made machine gunner.

One morning, after I had been with the squad four or five days, we were told to move out of our foxholes—with everything. I was carrying two tin boxes of ammo, of course. It was snowing, and we walked and walked. God, it was heavy. After you carried the ammo about ten miles, it seemed like it weighed tons.

When we reached where we were going, we came on an old Korean man, walking toward us, covered with blood. He was looking for someone to help him. Everyone was ignoring him, walking right by.

Finally, we had to climb a mountain and dig in—in all that snow. We stayed up all night in those holes, practically froze, and, of course, I didn't have the slightest idea from which way the Chinese would come, if they did come. Just completely confused. Not the slightest idea what was going on, what we were supposed to be doing, where we were going or who was out front. Just complete confusion. The whole war was like that.

There was no fighting until the next day when we were ordered out of there to another spot. We were on a low place and they were higher, firing down on us. We returned a little bit, not much. I fired a few shots. Anyhow, we withdrew again. The Army principle was to just fire—just shoot, just keep bullets flying. That's so completely different than my idea of shooting. My idea was to make every bullet count. I'd picked this up from childhood—don't shoot until I see something and when I shoot, I know I'm going to get it. And that was my principle in the Army and that's why I was always being more or less castigated.

In March, I fought in Operation Killer, when we understood that we were not to take any prisoners. Once, we had seized two Chinese prisoners—all shot to pieces, but they could still walk. We were all standing around and a lieutenant passed the buck and just walked off. So the sergeant looked around and said, "Well, who's going to do it?" No one spoke. I certainly didn't; I mean, I just couldn't. I turned my back and walked off a little bit. But there were two kids about my age; they volunteered—just to show they were manly, I suppose, because no one else had the stomach to shoot those two helpless men. They shot them right there. One died pretty easily, but they had to empty a whole clip into the other's head before he quit moving.

On March 11 came one of our first heavy fire fights with the Chinese. We were ordered to take this high mountain, on top of which the Chinese had machine-gun nests. We attacked early in the morning, and this Chinese machine gunner was up there, shooting down. He caught our platoon sergeant, right in the stomach, first burst. I was the machine gunner now and I set up and tried to draw his fire. His burst hit right under the barrel of my gun. Our first three squads went up and I gave them cover. They took the peak with bayonets.

We moved along the ridge. The Chinese had a chain of positions. I was up in front shooting the machine gun from the hip whenever I could. We had almost taken the last of it and were under fire behind some rocks when our own artillery fired on us. The first shell landed right on the head of a man in the second squad. Just blew him apart, and part of his brains landed on my shoulder and my helmet. I was just there helpless, with these shells exploding all around us. I was saved only because I was behind that rock. I was shocked more than any other time. We lost five men in my squad alone. I was saying: *If this is it, well, it's it.* I was hoping: *God, don't let it kill me.* I prayed: *For God's sake, let me make it through this.* Half the platoon was either wounded or dead, right there. The rest of us had to go on. All the rest of that day, we continued fighting. A shot went straight through my canteen on my hip. That night, we sat there with nothing to eat, no water to drink. We just sat there all that night.

By the next morning, I was ready to drink anything. We went down to the bottom, and there was a spring. We all made a dive for it. I had been carrying the gun for a while, and I was just laying it against a little bush, when a friend shouted, "Wills, look out!" I looked, and there was a little piece of wire running to a booby trap hooked right to that bush. As I jumped back, it went off. It caught me standing up.

Ripped my left thigh and knee open. Some people were hit in the face. I managed to drag myself out of the mud. Medics got to us, and one started cutting my trousers. They were all soaked with blood, and he cut up to the knee and saw all my thigh ripped open and said "Jesus Christ!" and right away gave me a shot. It made me feel good; I just lay back and thought: *All right, I've got my million-dollar wound. I'm getting out of here. I can get something to eat and something to drink.*

They carried me out on a stretcher and onto a Jeep. I got a drink of water and was on my way out. I didn't care. I was glad to be wounded, just to get away from that. Then the Jeep driver said, "You've made it this far. You'd better hope you'll make it the rest of the way. This road is mined." That started me praying again.

I was taken by Jeep and plane and train all the way back to Pusan. I was hoping to make it to Japan, but by the time we reached Pusan at midnight, my leg had started getting red and infected. So they ordered me off the train and put me in the Swedish Red Cross Hospital. Everyone else went on to Japan.

As soon as I got to the hospital, they took everything away, clothes, pistol, everything; all I managed to salvage was my wallet. They stripped me in front of a nurse. Of course, I was terribly embarrassed; that was the first time I'd ever been compelled to strip in front of a woman. I'd never been so embarrassed in all my life. Those Swedish Red Cross nurses were pretty, you know.

They X-rayed me and operated on me at two that morning. They never got all the shrapnel out; I've still got some in there. The leg had to drain and I had to go back and get about twenty-five stitches in my left hip. Then I had to learn to walk again. I stayed in the hospital close to a month.

When I finally got out, I was sent to the 8069th Replacement Depot, and then came one of the points in my life when my whole destiny wavered for a minute or two.

I met a friend who was a guard there, and he said I should get a guard's job too. I went to see the sergeant of the guard who told me he needed some men, but was I willing to serve an extra six months? I was nearly ready to be rotated after six months in Korea, but I told him that didn't matter. So he sent me to the first sergeant. He was busy on the phone, and I waited and waited, and finally he said I should come back in the morning. His attitude annoyed me, so I said the hell with it and I didn't go back.

A few days later, I was shipped back to the fighting. I met three buddies, and we were going back together, but two of them were going to jump the train and shack up with some Korean girls on the value of their baggage. They wanted me to do this, too, but I told them I was going to get my time over with and get out of Korea.

I got back to my old company just after my eighteenth birthday on May 3. Things were all changed. Most of the people I had known were gone. I was made gunner again. We got into a couple of small battles before the big one when they captured me on May 18.

This last big battle for me started when we were ordered up on Hill 755. By the time we got there and got our holes dug, it was five in the afternoon. My position was just down from the peak a little bit. Everything was quiet. Suddenly we got the call that they were on their way. The Chinese had concentrated in a forest across a little swayback ridge. Things started. That night they charged us five times.

It was pitch dark up on that mountain and I got into a hell of an argument with a sergeant. I wouldn't fire the machine gun until I was certain I saw someone and knew I was going to hit him. The sergeant was shouting, "There they are—out there—the shadows, you see them. Shoot!" And I'd tell him, "I don't see a damned thing; there is not a thing out there." He was practically hysterical.

He told me to get out, he'd do the firing. So I stepped aside and he started shooting, just sort of wildly. The platoon leader came running down and chewed him out right then and there. The two gunners above us ran out of ammo and their barrels burnt up. We were ordered up there.

We never made it to the top. The Chinese had seized the high ground and were firing down on us. I set up fast just under the crest and was firing up. In front of me was a foxhole with a GI in it. He tried to get out. One of my tracers hit the ground and started burning there and lit up the whole area. Just as it did, this GI jumped out of his foxhole to dash back down the hill. When he did, practically everyone on our side, everyone on the other side too, saw him and shot. People didn't know who he was. He got shot down by both sides. I can still see that sight. I knew him; his nickname was "Red."

We never retook that hill. We got a radio message saying that the company on the left and the company on the right had already withdrawn and ordering us out immediately. We really fled that place.

I had my .45 out, and we were racing down this path and, just about halfway down, ran into a group of Chinese coming up the side to cut us off. There was a fire fight, right there, like one of those old Western movies. Right there in the middle of the path; no more than about twelve feet apart. I must have hit three or four. They started throwing hand grenades and threw one right at me. I jumped over the side of the hill—a steep drop—and this hand grenade came rolling right behind me. My tripod caught on a vine. I gave the tripod a jerk; it wouldn't come loose, and I let it go and kept on sliding, and the grenade went off behind me. I kept sliding and finally gained my feet and I couldn't slow down and ran into a log so hard I still have a dent in my shin. When I hit the log, I went head first, lost my helmet and the clip out of my pistol. I was stunned. Finally, I could move and dragged myself to the bottom. There everything was so confused, and so many people had been lost that we just organized a sort of secondary line.

The next morning, we reorganized and marched again, climbed all day and got on top of a mountain. I had given my .45 to a wounded fellow who was going back and had picked up a rifle. We had no sleep, nothing to eat, nothing to drink, our canteens had been long empty. We were three days without sleep and two without food or water. Just fighting and moving, trying to stop the big Chinese spring offensive.

We got orders to turn around and come back. Back we came. It took hours to get to the road again. We were loaded on trucks and shifted to a ridge near the 38th Parallel where the French were withdrawing because there were so many Chinese out front. As the French came down, they told us, "You're crazy going up there. You'll never get out again." And they were right.

We climbed single file up the path and found their old positions. We had no idea what the terrain was like or where we were going, up those winding paths. As we moved up, the leader of a machine-gun squad just dropped in with the French line and walked right out. I never saw him again. By the time we got up the hill, the platoon leader made me squad leader. I was squad leader for about four hours, that's all.

The Chinese attacked, and we had a hell of a fight there. Everything was confused; nobody knew where anyone was. Then we were surrounded on three sides. On the way up the hill, we had been told to remember the path in case we had to fall back. Now, when we were driven off, there was one large group behind me carrying wounded, and I was up front with four or five others, scouting the path. We got strung out, and the first thing I knew, I was all by myself. I was on the side of a steep hill, which dropped off sharply to the right for about six feet to a little stream. It was pitch dark—no moon —one o'clock in the night. Far ahead of me, I could see our searchlights, behind our lines. Far behind me was the sound of firing. Alone, I was going down the narrow dirt path, when I heard some noise up ahead. It sounded like firing. I went a little more and stopped, went a little more and stopped. I heard talking and jumped off to the side of the path and waited about a half hour in the bushes. Not a sound. Finally, I got up and continued on down. I walked up to within three feet of a little curve in the path. Suddenly a man stepped out of the bushes. I could see he was Oriental and from his uniform, I thought he was South Korean. He came up to me and offered me his hand. I thought: *Everything is all right; only a South Korean would do that*. So I slung my M-1 on my shoulder.

As soon as I did that, another man stepped out from the other side and grabbed my rifle. I grabbed it at the same time. Three or four more stepped behind me with Russian submachine guns and brought their muzzles up next to me. They took the rifle away from me and led me around the curve, and there were a dozen other guys I knew. The Chinese had already captured them. And that was it.

III

DEATH MARCH

The GI's ahead of me had made it out before the Chinese closed the path. The main group behind me took another path and escaped. It was a matter of a few minutes. Just that much difference and I was a prisoner.

We sat there fifteen or twenty minutes. We heard fierce firing back down where they had caught me. I could make out a Browning automatic rifle and some Chinese shots. Then another few minutes and they brought up two more GI's. One of them told us they had come down with another fellow from my unit, an ex-Marine, and when the Chinese tried to take this former Marine's BAR away, he shot a Chinese right in the eye. Then he fired at the others and raced back down the path. They shot him in the back. He died on the spot.

I sat there hungry and tired and thirsty—just fed up with everything. Some of the other GI's were scared, and told me: "Put up your hands. Keep your hands up. Otherwise, they'll shoot." I didn't care. If they want to shoot me, all right, shoot me, I don't care. I wouldn't put my hands up. I wasn't going to beg.

The Chinese found some .45 pistol ammunition in my pocket. They wanted to know where the pistol was. I tried to explain with gestures that it was still up on the hill somewhere. I had a hard time. They thought I was hiding it somewhere. All I could do was point up the hill.

Just about this time, our people started an artillery barrage. Down it came, all around us. I just sat there and didn't care. If it got me, it got me. But the Chinese got very excited —shouting and hollering—and moved us through my battalion headquarters area, which they had taken with all our trucks, Jeeps. It was a smoking ruin. On the way they made me carry a Russian rifle for them; some of the others carried extra things too. They kept my M-1. They stuck us all in a little Korean house and kept us squeezed in there almost till dawn.

Just before it got light, they came and asked who could drive, and some of us said we could. So they took us back to the battalion area and wanted us to drive the Jeeps and trucks that would run. We got them started. Mine had a trailer on it. We were thinking, maybe we'll get to drive all the way north and won't have to walk. But we came down the slope into a large stream and the first vehicles got stuck. I never got that far. It was getting light and dangerous, so they took us back to the hut. I did manage to grab a gray blanket out of the Jeep I had been driving. I rolled it up and tucked it under my arm.

The Chinese took us up the side of a mountain and kept us there all day. I finally got something to eat. Another GI had an extra can of cold hamburger and gave it to me. I ate it bit by bit, spent about twenty minutes eating it. I never forgot that can of hamburger.

We were all in a state of shock. We didn't know how much longer we were going to live. They might kill us, I thought. Or we might just die from lack of food. Or we might get killed by our own men. This was the beginning of the process by which we would lose all our standards.

That night, they took us back down the hill to that little Korean hut and we got our first food from them: water with a few grains of sorghum, like we fed cattle at home. It came in a wooden trough, like you feed pigs from. It was a hot thick liquid, a dull pink color, and at the bottom was about an inch of sorghum. I filled my canteen cup with this water with about twenty grains on the bottom. That was supper. And that's the way it was for the first week or so. A little bit of this gruel and maybe a few weeds they had picked and cooked.

They stuffed us all back into this little hut, and at about ten that night they came back and moved us out and started marching us north, picking up other prisoners along the way. The group grew to at least fifty GI's. Some were wounded. We walked all that night into early dawn. Then we stopped and ate some more of that stuff. A lot of the men wouldn't eat it—wouldn't even attempt to eat it.

This became the routine. We would be hidden under trees during the day and I would sleep on my blanket. By night we walked, going north. They fed us once in the morning and once at night—this same stuff. We picked up more captured GI's until there must have been three hundred. There were armed Chinese guards spotted along the column. Of course, our Air Force bombed night and day. Whenever the Chinese guards heard a plane, they would shout and fire their rifles into the air as a warning. The first Chinese word we learned was the word for "air raid." Then everyone would stop and lie down off the side of the road.

During those first terrible days of this death march, we were always looking for a chance to escape. I kept an eye on the guard—looking for a chance to slip off or fall down and hope he would walk by. This was foremost in my thoughts for the first week or two. But I never got a chance. A few did try; one or two were shot, and the rest were caught and brought back. The farther north we got, the more remote any chance of escape became.

Now the desire for food was building up. An animal desire for food. You just had to have it. Anything. You would march along with your eyes closed and think about it. Your mouth waters. Then you start thinking about all the different things you've eaten, how to cook them, how they were made, what you'll eat when you get back. And this goes on and on and on. You get visions of wonderful food: baked macaroni with cheese, spaghetti and meat balls, lemon meringue pie, Boston baked beans and brown bread with butter soaked in it. The thing I thought most of was a frozen malt—a frozen vanilla malt.

A lot of people wouldn't eat the stuff the Chinese gave us: dry cooked red grain with maybe a few hard wild weeds on top. Later on, of course, they died. There was an expression: "Giveupitis." A lot of people died because of that. Mentally, I gave up too; but physically, I knew that if I didn't eat something, I was going to die. It was like swallowing a bowl of sand, spoonful by spoonful. This food gave you awful cramps. The indigestion was terrible. Every day, every night. You'd have to move around to get the gas up. It burns and burns and burns.

The people who wouldn't force the food down were mainly people from the city. There would be little worms in our sorghum. If it was cooked dry, you didn't notice them and ate them. But in the mornings the sorghum frequently was cooked soupy, so you would take your little flat Korean metal spoon and scoop off the worms floating on top.

For weeks, this was our routine. We would sleep on the hills in the daytime under the trees. At night, we just dragged along and dragged along in the darkness. No washing, no shaving. You were lucky if you got enough water to drink. My green fatigues were filthy. If your boots came apart, you walked barefooted. Mine held up.

One morning they stuffed us all in a tunnel dug into the side of a hill. I suppose it had been a mine. They forced us to crawl down into it. There was about a foot of water in it, and Chinese troops must have used it for cover because it was littered with piles of excrement. I was unlucky because I was one of the first ones in and had to go clear to the end. I sat on my helmet to keep out of the water. It was black, and there we sat. After a couple of hours, someone tried to light a cigarette, but the match wouldn't light—no oxygen—and we panicked, felt we couldn't breathe. We'd suffocate in here!

As the hours passed, the panic built up, and the people in the rear started pushing toward the opening. It almost came to the point where the Chinese were going to start firing in at us. We were gasping for breath. I realized the best thing to do was just sit still and use as little effort as possible. But things became so bad the Chinese finally saw they had to let us out or shoot us all. I just managed to get to the opening, dragged myself there. And when I caught a breath of fresh air, a sudden pain hit me—a tremendous, dizzy headache. I could barely walk. But the guards got me moving again—prodding me with their rifles and yelling.

We were a ragged bunch of soldiers—hungry, dirty, unshaven, usually in pain. We were mostly Americans, a few British, a few Dutch, a few Turks. Everyone was just trying to exist—to survive. No one was able to take charge. Every value you ever had, every standard, is slowly crushed. Money is completely useless. I've seen men burn it up, use it for toilet paper. Tobacco, salt, something to eat, that's the only thing that has value. A grain of tobacco becomes more precious than a five-dollar gold piece. Men would fight over a quarter-of-an-inch cigarette butt. They would fight over a spoonful of rice. You became an animal.

After two or three weeks, people began dying. We would wake up many mornings and see two or three dead. They had to be buried; it was only decency that it should be done, but you couldn't—you didn't have the energy. The Chinese guards would pick out the stronger prisoners and make them dig at bayonet point. Very often, the guards had to finish the hole themselves.

You really can't worry about the other fellow; you are just at the line of existence yourself. If you go under that, you die. You would help each other if you could. Most would try; I wouldn't say all. I remember one fellow trying to carry another. He carried him maybe a hundred yards and couldn't go on. He had to leave him. Most all those who were left behind didn't show up again.

38

For all of us, each day seemed like a year—the nights even longer. You didn't live unless you tried; if you didn't try, you died. I've always been stubborn, very stubborn. Maybe it's something I developed in my childhood—sort of a stubbornness to keep going to the very last.

I remember one night early on the march, going through a strategic pass. The road was just teeming with milling Chinese and mules and mule carts all going in different directions—terrible confusion. We had to run awhile, then stop, run again and stop. All in the dark. I just managed to get through the pass when a plane came over. The guards fired their rifles and we were ordered to lie down on the side of the road. I threw myself in a little ditch and prayed. That's all you can do. The plane dropped flares, very white, eerie. The whole area lit up; it was frightening. You hear the high shrill shriek of the bombs coming down. Then all sound stops—and there is a tremendous bright flash. You feel the blast, and shrapnel goes zinging through the air. A number of GI's got hit. The worst was one man who had his foot badly injured. He was just put on the side. I don't know what ever happened to him. When someone got wounded or fell sick, that was more or less the end. Very few reappeared.

Sometimes a night fighter would come over and strafe. Any sort of a truck or a running motor was dangerous to be near. We came to fear those things. Whenever a truck came near our line, everyone would curse it and hope it would get away from us quick.

We came to a little deserted village in the foothills and we stayed there and rested for about a week. It was peaceful. We'd go out and sit under the pines; the sun warmed us. Sort of an end to all that suffering. It was wonderful to be able to do just nothing. We were put into squads and platoons and we organized the division of the food for our squads. The food seemed better. Each squad was given two pans, and two men would go from each squad to pick up the food and then divide it among the men. Two different men each meal. Everything was measured—very carefully, by spoonfuls, and if it was beans, bean by bean. Everyone would stand there with his canteen cup or a tin can, and watch. And much later on, when we began to get bits of meat, you might get a sliver the size of a match, but it was important. I've seen people fight over one sliver—many times. That piece of meat seemed like a matter of life and death.

While we were there, we had a chance to write our first letter. They gave us those air-letter things with a peace dove on it. There was a great discussion whether it was a propaganda trick but eventually most people did write. I wrote about three lines—said I'm still alive. I addressed it to my father, but my family never received it.

When it came time to move out, it took a tremendous effort to get us up and out of there. A few had to be left behind. We were still haggard and thin, dirty, filthy. We knew it meant all that suffering on the road again.

One afternoon right after this, I discovered my first louse crawling on me. I'd had this itching around my ankles and waist and scratched and developed little sores. Of course, in our state, a sore wouldn't heal. The louse sickened and frightened me, because we had been told about diseases that lice carry, and we knew that the smallest thing wrong with you, that was it. You couldn't recover. A number of people developed dysentery and they died.

Then our battle with the lice began. They are little white and black insects about the size of a match head. They get in your seams and every place. So twice a day I pulled off my clothes and went through all the seams. You find them and kill them. When you press them, they snap. But they aren't dead yet—you've only broken their sac in the rear. You've got to crush the head to kill them. Otherwise, they'll just kill you, eat you up. Those who didn't bother to find them and kill them would die.

One night in July, when we'd practically nothing to eat for two months and some were dying off, we reached the lowest stage of our physical endurance. It had been raining for two days. It was raining this night, and there was about a foot of mud. We slouched and slopped along. We were filthy anyhow. We were going through another mountain pass. Soaked through, mud, Chinese guards shouting and hollering, trying to move us along a little faster. Great confusion and a line of Chinese coolies bringing supplies the other way. American bombers overhead dropping flares and bombing the road. Just one continuous line of shouting people with horses and mules and everything. We reached the top and stopped for a break.

I just dropped—right down in the mud. I didn't care. We all reached that stage where nothing mattered. In fact, if you died, that was better. I lay there thinking of food. I could just see it—laid on a nice table with a clean white tablecloth, a glass of water, some nice silver. And I lay in the mud, filthy, with all this noise and confusion going on around me.

When the order came to move on, getting up took the greatest effort I've ever made—getting out of that mud and moving again. You didn't want to. It was a terrible effort just to make yourself stand up and move on. But I knew that if I didn't, that was the end of the line. In the dark, quite a few didn't get up.

After a while we came to a mining camp, a small village in a very deep valley. They put us in some old Japanese barracks on the side of the hill overlooking the village, and we stayed there about three weeks. Each man was given a little space on the wooden floor, elbow to elbow. I made friends with a soldier from Florida, an older fellow who had been in the Coast Guard, and shared my blanket with him. We'd pick lice together out of our clothes every morning and every afternoon. It became a little ritual. And we shared food. Now a number of people were doing this, in groups of two or three.

Here in the mining camp, we would frequently find seven or eight men dead in the morning. It was common to wake up and find the man next to you dead. We didn't have anything to do, and just because we didn't have to make an effort, people wouldn't get up. They wouldn't try. They just let themselves die. Again a lot of them wouldn't force the food down. People born and brought up in the city gave up easiest. There was less feeling of hunger now, and you had to make an effort to eat, to get this stuff down. My weight dropped to maybe a hundred pounds—I'm about two hundred now. Before we got to the prison camp on the Yalu, I suppose about a third of the men died. More of them died in the mining camp than on the road.

It was the Turks who came through this the best. They had one officer with them and he was a god; his word was absolute law. The Turks were disciplined; not one died. The British and Filipinos were also organized. The Americans were the least well organized. We had some officers with us, but they didn't take charge. An officer would order you to do something, and you'd just tell him to go to hell. Both of you felt you would probably never make it back.

After a few days, the Chinese came around and said they needed people to wash the rice or sorghum. I figured that I had to keep in motion as much as possible; that was the only way to keep alive. So I volunteered with about six others. We became a special squad. We lived next to the kitchen. We got a little more to eat, and this sort of conditioned me.

Twice a day, very early in the morning and again in the afternoon, the Chinese led us down into the village where the stores were kept in the back of an old Korean woman's house. Later, they more or less trusted us and allowed us to go down and come back on our own. We washed the stuff at the village well and carried it back up the hill by a flight of about a hundred stone steps. I had to force myself to do it, but at least I wasn't just sitting on the hard floor all day long.

After a couple of weeks, the Chinese collected all our clothes into huge piles and issued us Chinese uniforms, and the Korean women in the village washed our clothes. They brought them back and dumped them there when I was out on the food-washing detail. Of course, everybody just helped themselves. When I came back, there wasn't a thing left for me or the others. They had to let us keep our Chinese uniforms. Mine didn't fit me; the trousers came about halfway up my legs. But I wore Chinese clothes from then on.

The Chinese guards weren't brutal to us. Generally, they were indifferent. They were disciplined troops, not "Chinese People's Volunteers", as Peking called them. That was a lot of nonsense. They were disciplined, regular Red Army troops.

We started getting a little square box of tobacco, made in China, every once in a while. I didn't smoke, so I gave mine to my friend from Florida or traded it for sugar, later on when they started giving us a sugar ration which amounted to three tablespoons a week. I would keep the blue cardboard box that the tobacco came in. A few collected their boxes together and made little decks of cards. Those were the most enterprising; of course, that was the wisest thing to do. But most didn't do it. I would turn mine inside out and on the inside I would write down all the delicious food I was going to eat when I got back. I must have written down hundreds. A lot of people were doing this. I'd sit there and look at the list and go down each item. I could remember that I had eaten each one before and just how it had tasted.

One day an American was brought in who had escaped from a POW camp that had been there before us. Everyone was turned out, and he was given a perfunctory sort of public trial in front of us. I think that he had wounded or maybe even killed somebody during his escape. The Chinese said that he was guilty and decided that they were going to shoot him. They took him away, and we were told that he was shot. I didn't see it, but some of the others said they did.

There was still some talk in our group about escaping, but everyone was so weak that no one even attempted it. A couple of others who had escaped earlier were captured and brought back. After a kangaroo trial, they were punished by being placed in a wooden cage about three feet wide, three feet deep

43

and the height of a man. All you could do was to stand up in it. It's a terrible strain. You have to stand at attention. You can't move. There is a guard on you all the time and the instant you move, he pokes you with his bayonet. After a time, you just slump unconscious. They would take you out until you revived, and then put you back in again. Some were left in a cage like that for weeks.

I was never punished in the cage, but I got one chewing-out by the Chinese. When we first arrived at the mining camp, the Chinese had searched everyone thoroughly. We had to take off every stitch of clothing. They registered all money and anything of value, rings, pens, things like that. I had an old ballpoint pen, a very cheap thing, that I had bought in Pusan after I had been wounded. They registered that. I also had a lot of military script on me, but that was useless. In fact, I still have it; this old script from my last payday. And I had a silver dollar that I had kept with me as a good-luck piece. The Chinese collected our U.S. money and exchanged this silver dollar for ten units of Korean money.

A flourishing black market developed among the GI's and between GI's and the Korean villagers. The Chinese tried to stamp it out but they couldn't. The GI's managed to buy a few things in the village, candy, food and some soap. They also traded tobacco and some clothing. I traded my ballpoint pen to a GI for a ring he had. Then I sold the ring in the village for about fifteen units of Korean money. So I could buy a little candy now and then in town. You could buy a fairly good chunk of their licorice taffy for one bill.

The Chinese had inspections every so often and they found my pen was missing. They more or less knew what had happened to it, but when they asked me where it was, I claimed that I had lost it out of my pocket in the well while I was drawing water to wash the rice. A fairly decent excuse. They weren't going to send me down in the well to get it out. But they gave me a rough going over verbally. That's all that happened to me. I remember two GI's were bashed good by

44

the Chinese, verbally, for stealing onions in the village, and were made to stand at attention for hours. By this time a few were stealing in town and this sort of punishment was going on constantly.

All this time there was still hope that we would be freed, liberated. And, of course, there were always rumors. That's what kept us going: rumors. "They're only about eight miles south of here." "There's just been a landing north of here." "The paratroopers dropped over there." All of this constantly. Except for this hope, I expect most people thought they'd never make it out.

Before we had arrived, the camp had been bombed by an American plane one night. A 500-pounder had come through the tile roof of the cook house and lodged like a dart in a huge metal cooking vat. A GI cook, who was sleeping by the vat, wasn't even hurt. The bomb didn't go off. The prisoners who were there at the time couldn't disarm the bomb—the mechanism had been jammed by the impact—so they gingerly pulled it outside and leaned it against the barracks. It was there when we arrived, and we sort of kept one eye on it with great respect.

It took a tremendous effort to get us organized and out of the mining camp. Quite a few had to be left behind. The longest trek was from there north to the Yalu. Again we walked at night and slept during the day on the side of hills or in the fields. We had to reach certain designated places every night. Frequently, we couldn't make it, and the sun would catch us still on the go. Because of that, we were strafed numerous times by American planes. Once we dashed into a railroad tunnel for protection, and the planes tried to blast the openings with us inside. Another time we had bedded down in Korean houses in the late afternoon; five of us were on a porch between two sections of a house. Not more than ten yards away under some bushes were two camouflaged trucks. Fighters started attacking the trucks; we thought they were attacking the house. I remember these planes coming right at the

45

houses. I could see the rockets and the muzzles of the guns firing, smoke from the guns and then the rockets coming. The guard wouldn't let us move. When the planes finally flew off, we were allowed to sit up and we saw both those trucks on fire, flaming like hell.

We would watch dogfights every day—Sabres against MIG's, and we would cheer the Americans on. Once, some U.S. jet fighters caught us in the open. There was absolutely no place to hide. So we started waving at the planes, and they flew around us two or three times and then flew off. They must have realized who we were.

As we got farther north, we saw more and more Russian trucks. Near the end, the Chinese marched us right into the city of Sinuiju near the top of the west coast of North Korea. The people lined the roads to see us coming in, looking like abominable snowmen—huge beards and long hair. We never shaved till we got to the prison camp. We didn't care, didn't have any feelings. It didn't matter.

At the outskirts of the city, we walked by big ack-ack batteries manned by Russians. A Russian truck with Russians on it stopped on the road as we walked by. One man in our platoon could speak Russian; he had been a Russian immigrant. He told us that was Russian lettering on the truck and he shouted to them in Russian, and they asked him who he was and where he came from. They said they were Russians and this was their ack-ack battery, and they gave us chunks of black bread and some cookies. I got a cookie.

During the march the Chinese didn't try much to convert us politically. They claimed they were volunteers and told us we were working for Wall Street. I'd never taken notice of Wall Street, but the Chinese said we were "workers of America" and that we had been deceived by the capitalists. But they were saving the indoctrination for later.

North Korea is rugged country. For weeks we climbed—mountain after mountain after mountain. We just wanted to go to the top of the next mountain. It was pure agony. We would get to the top, hoping for level land, and there would be another mountain on the other side. First, we would have to get down this mountain and that hurt more than going up; it hurt in the knees. Our legs were only about the size of my forearm now. Each time we would get to the top, hoping: Let there be a level stretch on the other side of this mountain. But there never was.

At long last, on the morning of October 8—almost five months after I was captured—we, the survivors, came into a small level valley surrounded by mountains. At the far end was the camp.

This was the northwest tip of Korea. At first, none of us believed it was the camp. It looked like another large Korean village. So we came down this long road, thinking we'd spend another day here and then move on. Until we got almost to it. Then we saw some GI's. We were elated. This was the end of the march, the end of the mountains, the end of our journey.

Our feelings spun around 360 degrees. Nothing more to worry about. We would just sit the war out here and rest.

There was not a person among us whose ribs you couldn't count. Our knees were knobs; our faces hollow; our beards shaggy. We wore lice-infested rags. We dragged ourselves into camp.

IV

DECISION

Camp One had been a Korean village at the northwest tip of the country, very near the Yalu. As we straggled in, the GI's saw us coming and gathered around. They had been here a half year or more and the first thing everyone wanted was news of what was going on. We could give them news only up to last May, but that was more recent than anything they had had. And we wanted to know what conditions were like, about food, clothing, medical care. Then the Chinese lined us all up, and after a long time finally got us situated in the mud houses. There was no wire around the camp. They just had guards posted.

The long march had beaten us down, made us into animals struggling to stay alive. I was put in a squad with nine others, and we all occupied one room less than twelve by twelve feet in a mud house. We slept on mats on the floor with our heads to the walls and all our feet in the middle, and there wasn't room for any passage between us. Our squad got along pretty well. In some squads they had fights every day. I don't think we ever had any fights in ours.

Slowly, our food began to improve; there were bits of pork in the side dish, which you had with the rice, and frequently turnips; and more rice and some steamed bread, and we started getting bean curd and sometimes fried bread. So we started building up again physically. At the end of our stay, much later, we were getting far more meat than we could eat.

Soon, it started getting cold, and the Chinese issued us those blue-cotton padded uniforms. They were very warm, but you wear them throughout the winter, and by spring, they are so stinking and filthy you can hardly live with them.

Right after we got to camp, the Chinese asked everyone to write home and say we wanted peace in Korea. Everyone did this but in such a way that no one back home would believe it. I tried to change my handwriting as much as possible; I slanted it the other way. And I used words which I wouldn't use normally and referred to things, like a hired man, that didn't exist.

I ruined my eyes in the POW camp. When I joined the Army, I had perfect eyes, 20-20. During the winter, when we didn't have any vegetables at all, better than half the camp would have night blindness. It was comical in a way but also pathetic. Every night, just before lights-out, there would be long lines of prisoners holding onto each other and going down to the latrine with one man in front who could see. My eyes aren't very bad, but when I look beyond ten feet, it's sort of blurred.

The extreme feelings began to disappear. The hope of being rescued was more remote and the fear that you were going to be shot or that you wouldn't make it through was also more remote. We started feeling better and put on a little weight. I had lost fifty pounds. For Christmas, we each got treats, including a whole dried fish. We hadn't seen this much meat in six months. I ate the bones and head and all. We sat around and sang songs; the Negroes led us in singing spirituals.

All this time we had not given the slightest thought to women or sex. You just didn't care. A Brigitte Bardot could have walked through camp, and nobody would have raised an eyelid. From the time I was captured till about May 1953 —for two whole years—I didn't think of a woman, didn't want one, didn't care. It was more or less the same with the others. Then, of course, from that time on, sex occupied our minds as much as food.

49

After that, a few POW's—whether they had formerly been queer I don't know—openly expressed homosexual desires. There were maybe four or five in our company of two hundred men. They let their hair grow and fixed up their clothes to look like women's blouses. At first, this was pretty revolting, but gradually, as more and more expressed this sort of thing, the men learned to live with it. And these people organized entertainment and set up a band and would dance with other GI's at a club we had, and gradually became more accepted.

Another thing happened. Some of the POW's found that marijuana was growing all around the camp. Every time they would go out on a wood detail, they would bring some back and smoke it. At first only a few people smoked, but then it suddenly swept the whole camp. I started smoking it, too, one rainy day when the others were sitting around smoking. It made you feel high and very reflective. Almost everyone enjoyed it and kept doing it. Later, when the Chinese found out, they clamped down. They were ruthless. If they found any marijuana, you got punished. They tried to stop us bringing it in but we managed to hide it. By the spring of 1952, it was very scarce; it got to the point where I was smoking stems.

There were more than a thousand POW's in Camp One. This was the most western camp along the Yalu and the newest. It was near a railroad junction which we couldn't see but which the Americans bombed every night. We could hear that and see the searchlights, bombers and fighters. They rarely hit the camp. Since the main road ran right through the camp, a truck going through one night was caught by a lone bomber which dropped fifty-odd antipersonnel bombs and a couple of 500-pounders. Some Chinese got killed and some wounded; one British prisoner was wounded and one American officer and a sergeant killed. The mud wall of our house caved in and we had to dig ourselves out. Later, they put up Red Crosses, and we weren't attacked after that.

At first we were a hodgepodge of prisoners, but the British were moved elsewhere and eventually the American officers were moved out. So finally we were only GI's there. Some of the Southerners got to scrapping with the Negroes, so the Chinese suddenly moved the Negro soldiers to another camp, too.

Life got organized. The Chinese set up a hospital just outside the camp. They organized us into sports teams. I played on the company volleyball team; our team was the best in camp and we even played other POW camps.

In time we made things a bit more comfortable. We built double-decker bunks to give us more room. I had a top bunk, and one afternoon I was lying there, just studying the ceiling, which was papered with old copies of the *Shanghai News*. Suddenly, I came upon an item that told about the 38th Infantry being more or less wiped out, and I discovered that it was a story about the night I was captured. It was quite a coincidence. The paper had been there for some time; I had just never noticed it. I cut out this piece of the ceiling with a knife that I had made out of the arch support in my combat boots. Many of us had taken the metal support out of our boots when they fell apart, ground it down and put a handle on it. It made a good knife. My boots had finally given way in the front, the sole separated from the uppers. One day in the early part of 1952, when it was freezing cold and we had nothing to put on the fire, one of the guys found my old boots and some others, started a fire with some paper and threw the boots on it. That kept us warm for the rest of that day. It was the end of my combat boots.

The Chinese started political training early. At first, they were stupid about it. They started out giving us long lectures. Every man had to make a little stool, and rain or snow, sleet or hail, winter or summer, we had to go outside—down in the square where we all could gather—and sit on our stools and listen to lectures that lasted for six hours and even longer.

The interpreting stretched it out. But this was traditional Chinese. Their soldiers did it, so the POW's could, too. And we did.

We just sat there freezing. You could feel yourself freezing. There were always attempts to get off, pretend sickness or something. The more attempts at this, the more ruthless they became, demanding that we be there.

At first, the lectures were on Russia, how Russia had had her revolution, how the workers lived there, boasting about how many bricks they could lay in a minute. Then gradually, they started giving lectures about China, her history, her revolution, how the foreigners mistreated the Chinese. They told us the U.S. was an imperialist country and wanted to dominate the world and that the Korean War was only part of a master plan. They taught that we were all ordinary workers and we had been deceived into fighting for the capitalists. Then they made us read and discuss the *Shanghai News*, other communist papers printed in English and eventually ancient copies of the *Daily Worker* from New York. They made us do this. If you didn't join in, you got the turnip bin.

This was a cellar in the ground with the front open, exposed to the cold. You could be condemned to live in the turnip bin for a day, two days, a week, depending on your crime. Some people froze their feet and hands in the turnip bin. Especially in winter, it was terrible to get condemned to the turnip bin. I came close a couple of times.

We had woodcutting details miles away from camp and each of us had to carry back a quota of wood to the camp over a certain period—a log at a time. But over a distance of ten miles they could only post a few guards, so we got a chance to meet some Koreans and trade with them. We had soap now and I traded some soap once for a bag of turnips. But I was unlucky. As soon as I got back to camp, they had an inspection and caught me with the turnips. They condemned me to the turnip bin, but it was so full then they couldn't put me in it.

The fellows in it had stolen scraps from the kitchen; mine was the lesser crime, so I got off.

By the spring of 1952, the Chinese began to realize they were achieving a completely wrong result. Everyone was hating the lectures and hating China and Russia even more. They also had us watch Russian movies. I remember the first one—model workers performing "heroic" tasks. It was ten or fifteen below zero, and they made us sit out there for about three hours, watching this damned Russian laying bricks. The Chinese were just stupid. They thought by doing this that overnight we'd become Communists. They didn't know it but they were conditioning us to resent Russians.

Every prisoner was thoroughly interrogated and made to write an autobiography. We had to do this three or four times. Of course, everyone lied like hell. Put down anything, made up fantastic stories—anything but the truth. I made up stories about how I'd been in completely different parts of the States. One of the places I said I had been stationed, guarding installations, was New Mexico. I had never been anywhere near the place—but this lie came back to haunt me later when China was beginning its nuclear program.

When they realized they couldn't cram communism down our throats, they became more subtle. They set up a library in each company with books in English—Russian books, communist pamphlets, the *Daily Worker*, communist magazines. They quit the lectures and instead set up study groups. These would be voluntary. They just left us alone. Well, for the first month or so, no one even looked at the library or went near the so-called study group place. And then, eventually, one or two or three, because there was nothing else to do, walked into the library.

Being a POW got to me. A great number of the POW's, especially among the Negroes, felt: All right, so I do live in a capitalist society; it's still better than communism. But I brooded over it. It was always on my mind. The best years of my life—there I was, sitting there, rotting away. Day after day, I'd sit in front of our shack and stare at the huge mountain right ahead of us. You couldn't see over it.

I felt they wouldn't get me out. I felt they were saying they had got a few suckers. They didn't care about us. I'm here suffering. While we were over here dying, the people running the thing didn't care whether they won or not. They're back over there; they can sit at home and have their wine, women and song, cars, and all this nice life.

When I joined the Army, they had asked me for my preference and I put down that I wanted to go into tanks and to go to Europe. I didn't want to be in the infantry and I didn't want to be in Korea. I was fed up before I even got there. And hiking up and down those mountains with the machine gun on my shoulders—every step of the way deepened my anger with the Army. This wasn't what I had volunteered for.

Just before I was captured, MacArthur was relieved. He was my idol. He wanted to go into China. He was the one who wanted to fight the war the way I felt it should be fought, with planes and bombs in China. When he was relieved, that angered me. Hell, it certainly didn't look like they were going to take any measures against China. Once I was captured, this feeling intensified a hundredfold, the feeling that they wouldn't go ahead and fight the war and win it. If we're going to fight this war, then fight it. Bring over what's necessary and go ahead and win it. If it means dropping an atom bomb, then drop an atom bomb.

The fact that we had old World War II weapons—rifles, old planes, old tanks, no new weapons—and the fact that they wouldn't use or even threaten to use the atom bomb angered me even before I was captured. And now I felt they wouldn't get me out. They don't care about us.

This kept building up and building up until it reached the point that you want to fight, you want to do something. But there is nothing you can do. You get completely disgusted and you begin to feel you don't care. You don't even care about going back. To hell with it.

By the end of 1952, this feeling created a vacuum in my mind. I was getting madder and madder because they weren't trying to win the war. And all the propaganda from the Chinese side said we were losing in South Korea. It didn't look like I'd ever get out of there. Not any of us. I just sort of disowned the whole thing, the whole U.S. Army, the U.S. Government.

I got interested in what the Chinese had to say and once they saw you were interested, they became more friendly. When people started going into the library, I did, too—just looking around, then reading a passage here and there, and then taking out a book. I had never heard of Marxism. As far as I can remember, Marx had never been mentioned in our school. He should have been; we ought to have been given a basic idea of his theories. There is absolutely no way of combating an argument in his favor unless you know something about him.

When I was in school, communism may have occupied about five minutes in our old history book. There ought to be a whole course on it—intellectual discussions, not just fanatical declarations. Current affairs courses should follow every move of the Chinese and Russians with background material.

Before I went in the Army, I didn't think the United States was such an awful place. I said the Pledge of Allegiance every morning in school. But if you argue with a Communist face to face, you've got to be able to explain yourself, because he can explain himself and his theories. If you can't explain yourself, you're going to lose out to him. He would hit you with the Negro problem, unemployment, poverty and crime. I couldn't explain a lot of these things. In the camp this happened constantly with everyone.

The more I read in the library, the more I was convinced: Well, by God, this is just the thing that is needed. Equality

55

for everyone. Everything organized, planned, secure. On paper, it looks very nice, especially to someone who doesn't know anything about it, and who is thoroughly disgusted with his own government for letting him get stuck there and not making an effort to get him out.

One day I dropped into the study group. There were others there. They were reading and asking questions and a Chinese instructor was answering them. If you didn't know anything about Marx, all you could do was ask questions. You couldn't refute what he said.

I started going there twice, three times a week. Each company had its own study group and there were always ten or so fellows at ours. And later on, they had us go up to the camp headquarters where there were better interpreters, and they would talk with us and be friendly. We had the privilege of going there when we wanted to.

I lived and got my food with the squad. At first, the other guys who didn't go to the study group didn't think much about it. Later on, some became rather antagonistic. But the Chinese found out who was antagonistic and sent them to another camp.

My views changed gradually—one idea at a time. It was a long process and took a long time. Of course, you battle with yourself off and on. At first, you don't want to believe the United States is losing the war. You don't want to believe that they aren't going to liberate you. But after two years as a POW, you have long ago given up hope of being rescued and the war being won. You give in to those realities. Then you search for something else, something to stand on.

I can remember one evening when one of the political instructors called me over to his room. It was after dark and I took a seat on one of his hard, wood chairs with just a bare light bulb in the room. It was very cold. I was in my cotton-padded uniform with my hands tucked up into my sleeves to keep warm.

He started talking to me about the States. I tried to defend it as much as possible. He worked up to an attack gradually. He talked about how an American becomes President and he said, "Of course, it is only the rich that are able to become President." I told him that is nonsense, that anyone could become President. He said I was sadly wrong, that a poor man wouldn't stand a chance. I took the example of Lincoln, but he said Lincoln had rich supporters. Then he told me about the Republican Party and the Democratic Party. Now, he's telling me things that I don't know. He is telling me about all the money it takes for those conventions and everything. There wasn't much I could say because he was more or less right. The money had to come from someplace. Then all you can do is sit and listen. It breaks you down—bit by bit.

I did things I regretted later. We all did. I signed peace appeals in Camp One and in China later—peace appeals mainly directed against the United States—on the Korean war and later in China opposing U.S. intervention in Vietnam. Either they were sent to the United Nations or to people like Bertrand Russell, and they would urge that the war stop immediately and be settled on Chinese terms. The appeals said that the U.S. started the Korean War and was keeping the war going and demanded that the U.S. end the war. The Chinese platoon instructor would call in each man, one by one, and give him a long story and urge him to sign so the war could be stopped and you could go home. You couldn't really refuse to sign but I won't say everybody did; a few didn't. I signed many of the peace appeals. Now I wish I hadn't and am ashamed of it.

But except for signing those appeals and making some recordings there's nothing I can think of that hurt anyone in Camp One. I was friendly with the Chinese, but I wouldn't and didn't do anything that would hurt anyone else. Certainly, a number of people went through the study groups for what privileges they could get, and a number of them did tell the Chinese various things about men in their squads, maybe even making up stories. This did happen; but in my case, nothing like that happened.

The germ-warfare thing was pretty big. The first I heard of it was when the POW pilots made their statements accusing the United States of committing germ warfare, saying they had flown missions with the germ-warfare containers and had dropped them. They made a pretty damning case saying what they had dropped, where they dropped them. At first, I didn't believe it. Later on, I came to think that it was a possibility, and at points, I probably did believe that they did it. The study group and propaganda brought me to this stage of wavering. At Panmunjom during repatriation, they may have asked me if I believed it, and I may have said I did or didn't. To this day I don't know. But I didn't sign any germ-warfare appeals. Actually, these propaganda things were no worse really than what some of the students have been doing in the universities here. In fact, not as bad, in some cases, as far as their propaganda effect goes.

I believe the Vietnamese Communists are using pretty much the same methods that were used on us in camp and later in China. The number of Americans who do change their views while in captivity, whether with the Chinese or with the Vietnamese, seems very small, but the Communists work under very hard conditions. If they are giving you nothing to eat, you're filthy day in and day out and the Chinese or Vietnamese are trying to convince you that their side is right, it certainly isn't a very favorable climate to work in. But two years can seem like twenty. Slowly it wears on you.

I filled the vacuum left by my becoming dissatisfied with my own government by taking an interest in China, Chinese and communism—by reading and by developing a friendship with the Chinese. It opened a way forward; I found another path out. Their system seemed a better replacement than what I had just come from. Maybe the American system was collapsing, rotting. Crime has always been a big thing; very often you see corruption in government. The Chinese always played these things up.

As I became friendlier with them, they more or less treated me like one of them. They called me by my first name. I could go down anytime and drink tea. I could pass the guard and the guard knew who I was. They would call me in and ask my opinions on how they should go about organizing sports meets or something like that. They would never ask me about disciplinary action. Their policy was to make as many as possible friendly and to protect those from any of the others who might try to harm them. I didn't get any better treatment, except maybe my punishment would have been lighter if I had gotten into trouble. In my squad I kept sort of friendly with everyone so that I never made anyone angry. I never tried to influence anyone else. That's the way I've always been.

Toward the end of our stay in Camp One, the Chinese named me leader of my squad because I was friendly with them. Then I was in a difficult position—in the middle, trying to keep on good terms with the GI's and with the Chinese. All the squad leaders were appointed by the Chinese; some of them were very "reactionary." They appointed the squad leader on the basis of a man's ability to keep the squad organized and keep the men from getting into trouble.

Before I was a prisoner, I thought China was a terrible tyranny where innocent people were shot and killed and put into prison. But what I got from them in camp was completely different. Everything was nice, sort of an orderly planned way for everyone to live together. So by December 1952 or January 1953 I felt that if I got the chance someday, I would like to go to China. I thought I'd like to visit the place.

One night I went in and told one of the instructors that I'd like to see China. I thought that if enough people wanted to go, they'd take us to China for a visit. He told me that was impossible. Still, the idea stuck with me and sort of grew, but I didn't mention it anymore.

59

In the spring of 1953 I got pleurisy and had to go to the hospital. The Chinese wanted me to stay there because by then I was considered one of the "progressives." Everybody tried to get into the hospital. I stayed about a month, but I was fighting with the Chinese to get back to the company. I wanted to get back especially to play on the volleyball team: I missed playing in the inter-camp Olympics because I was sick. They wanted to send me back with the sick and wounded who would be repatriated to the States first. At that point nonrepatriation had not been decided on, but they figured I'd still be friendly to China when I got home.

In the hospital I was friendly with some of the nurses. When I got back to the company, a number of people kidded me about it, especially because I knew a few words of Chinese. So later when I stayed behind to go to China, someone started the rumor, which I read in the papers, that I had married a Chinese general's daughter who was a nurse in the hospital. There was no basis for it at all. But it took me a long time to convince even my father that I wasn't married. Every once in a while he would write me and ask when I was going to send them a picture of the general's daughter.

That summer, the agreement was signed for voluntary repatriation. The Chinese came to me and asked me if I still wanted to go to China. I said I would certainly like to. They said that now there was a chance; I didn't have to be repatriated.

They explained that I would have to stay in a neutral zone for three months, and if I remained staunch, they would take me to China. There, they told me, I could do whatever I wanted to. If I wanted to work, I could work. If I wanted to go to school, they would send me to school. Back in the squad, I didn't tell anyone.

Of course, the others in the study group knew how I felt about China and the Soviet Union. I was sympathetic to communism. To me it seemed like a very orderly, systematic way of organizing society; no one was very rich and no one was very poor. Everyone shared equally, more or less. I wouldn't say I ever reached the level of a Communist, because a Communist is a very loyal, disciplined person—and I'm not very disciplined.

I know most of the GI's decided to go home, but I suppose that most of them thought more about cars and women, in the later stages, than they did about other things. I've always been stubborn; I thought about past grievances and the fact that I'd been left there to rot.

The Chinese called me in once or twice and we talked about my going to China, but I had made no decision. Then they called me in one afternoon early in August and said they would have to know for sure by the following morning whether I wanted to stay or wanted to go. They said it was up to me to volunteer. As the Chinese instructor was explaining this to me, he was studying me and my true feelings.

I hardly slept that night. Just lay there on my top bunk, considering everything. First, I remembered my family, my brother and sisters, my father. That was the hardest part to lay aside. Then, for a long time, I thought about my role in the Army, and I got over that by saying to myself that I had joined the Army on July 27, 1950, contracted for three years, and it just so happened that the war in Korea ended July 27, 1953, exactly three years to the day I had joined up: so I felt my three years were finished. Legally, of course, they weren't, but I got over that point by deceiving myself. I felt I had been misplaced and deserted by the Army.

One little thing that I remembered from my mother stuck with me. It was just a common ordinary thing. I remembered when I was young—maybe about ten—and she was listening to the World Series on the radio. The New York Yankees were playing the St. Louis Cardinals. I was sort of rooting for the Yankees because I was from New York State. She overheard me and said I should be ashamed of myself. She said I should be hoping that the Cardinals would win because they're the weaker club. She gave me the feeling that I should always support the weaker side. And I had grown up with the idea that America was invincible. In Korea, I always thought the Chinese were the weaker side. That is what made me so angry, that America had the absolute power and wouldn't use it to save us.

Then, I thought of my friends back home and my good friends in the camp and how they would take it once they found out that I didn't go back. I knew that some of my friends in the camp would probably consider it wrong, and certainly wouldn't like me for doing it. And I knew that there was a possibility that the Army would consider it desertion. But there again, I had a little ground to stand on: the fact that the U.S. Government had signed the armistice giving me permission to go wherever I felt like going. The Chinese made that point very clear.

I spent a long time thinking over what China was going to be like. That was hard to imagine, but I told myself that I was still young and liked to travel and I tried to think of myself as sort of an adventurer. This would be something different; not many people would be doing it.

Sometime early in the morning, I remember well, I gave myself five minutes to make up my mind—the final decision. At the end of that five minutes, I decided I would go. Then, I just put everything else aside; I wouldn't think about it anymore.

That morning I took my time getting ready and at about 8 or 9 I went over and told the platoon instructor, the one who knew me best, that I had decided I was going to stay, that it was final.

V

DEFECTION

On August 6, 1953, the instructor called me down and told me I was leaving that afternoon for Camp 5. The prisoners from Camp 5 had already been repatriated; we had seen them when they came through our camp on trucks. The instructor wouldn't even let me go back for my things. He got my baggage. He feared someone might give me a hard time or even assault me. It had reached that stage in the end. Some people in the camp had made it clear that they weren't going back, and the feeling was pretty strong that they were deserting.

I suppose you could call me a defector or a turncoat. But I wouldn't consider myself a deserter or a traitor because the U.S. had signed the agreement with the Chinese that gave me the right to go to China if I wanted to. I don't think that makes me a traitor. Add to that the way I was treated. All of us thrown in there and forgotten. They certainly didn't make an effort to free us. They deserted us. Left us there for two years while they were having their good time back home.

In my own mind at the time, after going through the Chinese ideological training, I didn't feel I was defecting. I felt I was still being an American, that I was only doing this so that someday I might be able to help America in a different way. That's the way I felt at the time. Maybe later on I would help to change the system. Of course, I don't feel like that now; I lost all that.

Only one other person came to China from my company in

Camp One—Pfc. Richard R. Tenneson [of Clark's Grove, Minnesota], who was captured the same day I was. And even he didn't know I was coming until we met at headquarters. There were more who would have come, but the Chinese kept it all very secret and as a result most people didn't even know that anyone was going to China. Certainly from our company there would have been four or five more and as many as twenty-five from the five companies in Camp One alone.

I had to see the company instructor. He wanted to make sure my decision was final. He said I must consider that in China I wouldn't have the material benefits that I would in the United States and that I'd have to be prepared to live a life with fewer material things. I told him that I knew China was poor and life there wouldn't be so grand as life in the United States, but that would not make any difference in my decision.

Then I was taken down to headquarters and eventually Tenneson and several from other companies straggled in. They put Tenneson and me and at least three others on an open Russian truck. Later, the other three were rejected by the Chinese. Tenneson had gone through this same process of change as I had, but he was very outspoken in camp and this made a lot of trouble for him. Once or twice they tried to get him at night. I had avoided being seen with him.

We left Camp One right after lunch. There were no guards on the truck, just a Chinese driver in the cab. Now we were being trusted for the first time—fully trusted. At about five or six we arrived at Camp 5 right on the south bank of the Yalu. You could see China across the river. Some Chinese instructors were waiting for us and, for the first time, they called us "Comrade."

We met the GI's from Camps 3, 4 and 5 who were going to stay and they were all calling each other "Comrade." (Camp 2 had consisted of allied officers.) It took me two or three days before I decided who I liked and who I didn't. There were three or four I didn't care for at all—rather loudmouthed, bragging. I made up my mind who I'd stay away from. There were twenty-seven all told: twenty-one GI's who eventually went to China; a Scotsman Andrew Condron, a British Marine who went with us, plus five GI's who didn't go.

We got two Chinese commanders. Commander Tien, a veteran Red Army commissar, was an old man with a bald head; he wore glasses and must have been at least sixty. Commander Chang was his subordinate. They arrived with very good interpreters and started organizing us into a compact group with a systematic training program. At the time I didn't realize it, but looking back I see it was a program to determine for themselves which persons could go through the three-month period in the neutral zone, as the armistice agreement required. And they were trying to determine whether there were any people in the group who might have been sent there to destroy the group.

This was my first experience with the Chinese technique of "criticism-and-self-criticism." Each man had to analyze himself and be analyzed by the group to decide if he was fit to be a nonrepatriate. Could he go through the three-month period and would he stay loyal to the group?

We began the criticism sessions by doing exactly what we were told. Each man explained before the group his reasons for wanting to go to China and his reasons for not wanting to be repatriated. Those who knew him in camp had to give their views on him. All the time the Chinese commanders were deciding whether a man was sincere or not. And we chose a group leader; we appointed Corporal Claude Batchelor [of Kermit, Texas], and Sgt. Richard G. Corden [of Providence, Rhode Island] was appointed assistant group leader.

Later on, after the three-month period was over, the two commanders told us how they had summed up each man at that point. They had marked me down as a rather conservative, quiet person who would probably make it through the three-month period without causing any trouble to the group and without having second thoughts about his decision. They classified me as a rich peasant because they knew from my autobiographies that my father owned about 175 acres of land. That's nothing here, but to the Chinese it's over a thousand *mou*—an unheard-of amount of land. My father wasn't considered a landlord because he didn't have people working for him. He was considered a rich peasant and since I was his son, I naturally fell into that category. Everyone must fall into some category.

But the Chinese, typically, had to make an example of someone. They found out that three men, including two from Camp One, had traded with some Koreans for marijuana. The Chinese called a dramatic emergency meeting at night and Commander Tien read the charges against the three men. By this time everyone was feeling very "progressive," that we were Communists and that everyone was a comrade and should conduct himself like a comrade. The Chinese insinuated that the three had been sent to disturb and break up the group and encouraged the rest of us individually to criticize the three men. They kept building this up and building it up until some of them were in tears—sobbing away. Finally, as the Chinese expected, these three men changed their minds and "voluntarily" said they wanted to be repatriated. The Chinese had a little party for them and said that they were still "peace fighters" and hoped they would go back and fight for peace and work for socialism in the States.

During this time in Camp 5, I felt that I was a member of the socialist community and very close to the rest of the group. I felt I should try to help everyone in the group ideologically as much as I could. I considered myself a peace fighter, and I wanted to do everything I could to keep peace in the world. I felt that socialism, and eventually communism, were far higher stages of development than capitalism. These strong feelings came out of my study-group experience back in Camp One. Although I did not think so at the time, I suppose you might say I was brainwashed.

At Camp 5 we were indoctrinated to make the group solid, to give us a sense of duty to the group leaders. The Chinese worked to instill in us a feeling that this was a struggle we had to go through. Only "heroes," only the best, would get through the neutral-zone period.

During the three months in the neutral zone, we would be under control of the Indian Army. We would be on our own; there was not supposed to be any contact with the Chinese. "Explainers" from the U.S. Army were supposed to get a chance to explain to each of us why he should return home. So in Camp 5 we had dry runs facing the explainers. We were ordered to cause confusion to keep the explainer from making his explanation. Do anything—sing, make noise, turn your back—anything to keep from listening to what he had to say. We should criticize American foreign policy, and America for being a warmonger.

I didn't know it at the time, but the Chinese had set up a group within our group. The ones I remember in the inner group were Batchelor, Corden and Sullivan [Sgt. LaRance Sullivan of Santa Barbara, California]. They arranged a system of coded light signals with this inner group so that the Chinese could have direct contact with us while we were in the neutral zone. The light signals were used at night a number of times. They also tried to train a mascot dog we had with us, an ordinary little mutt named Nonrepat, to carry messages back and forth, but that never worked. And Commander Chang was planning to shave off his hair and to work at the camp hospital as a coolie. He turned up there later on, but I never knew it until, near the end of the three months, I went to the hospital to get a tooth filled and there he was, telling me not to let the cat out of the bag.

The last night before we left for the neutral zone, the Chinese threw a real banquet with many courses and wines and liquors. All of us got soaked, just laid out; the Chinese did, too. Some of the fellows had to be carried back to their rooms; one man even set his bed on fire. Affairs like that were meant to draw us closer together, to consolidate the group, and to let all our feelings explode.

Early the next morning we were taken by truck for two days to Kaesong near the neutral zone. The dirt roads were gutted and rough; I've never been so sore in all my life. We stayed in a camp there for about a week and were taken to a lovely Korean bath house that certainly had been used by the rich. We had more meetings to prepare us for the explainers. If anyone indicated he was sliding back—interested in sex, for example —he would be reported by someone. That is how things are controlled so effectively throughout China. You are always part of a group and if there are twenty of you, the other nineteen are always watching you and you are always watching everyone else. You have to report everything; otherwise, you will be reported for not reporting. You've got to do it. That's why China hasn't fallen apart, why the people haven't revolted.

In the neutral zone we were placed in a special camp about two acres in size, up on a hill, and completely fenced in. It was the first time we had ever been fenced in since we were captured. As soon as we sighted the camp, we started singing. The Indians were there. We could see some American officers, and I remember the drivers of the American cars were all standing around together and when we sang the "Communist Internationale," they tried to sing "The Star Spangled Banner." But they couldn't finish it; they didn't know the words. We laughed and cheered.

We were placed in a barracks and settled into a routine. Slowly and one by one the members of the group went to the hospital, which was also surrounded by barbed wire, and stayed there. It got down to about eight or nine of us left in the barracks. I didn't know Chinese Commander Chang was in the hospital and had direct control of the group there.

Then, about halfway through our time there, we discovered the existence of the inner group. I didn't mind the fact that there was an inner group but I didn't like not being told about it. I resented that some were trusted more than I was. It caused dissension. The group was getting splintered now.

Two of the group decided to be repatriated. One was Cpl. Edward S. Dickenson [of Cracker's Neck, Virginia]. He slept next to me and used to play the guitar in the evenings, and we would sit around on the cots and sing. He faked a headache to get away from the group. And the other was Batchelor, whom the Chinese had regarded as the most "progressive" man in Camp 5. They had guided his appointment as group leader. He was a very nice, sincere person, but just before our time in the neutral zone was up, Batchelor received a letter from his Japanese wife, and at midnight he crossed over.

I did think about my decision some. But I'm stubborn. I'd made up my mind in camp and that was it. I wouldn't let it bother me much. I wouldn't think about it very much.

We kept making trouble for the Indians. We protested that their dentist was trying to influence the men to go home; we objected when Bibles were sent to our group. And the Chinese ordered us to kidnap the Indian officer in charge of our camp to force the Neutral Nations Repatriation Commission to come down and accept our protests in person. We had a lot of argument over that. I thought it was rather stupid, and I was one of those who opposed it. I did not realize the orders for this came from the Chinese. But finally Batchelor got a majority to support the plan, and I said I'd have to go along with it.

Several of the group lured the officer into one of our buildings and wouldn't let him out. When our men grabbed him, the Indians put up machine guns around the camp and drew up a tank. It took the Neutral Nations Commission several hours to get there. Finally, we presented our petition to them and released the man.

None of us went to the shacks to see the explainers. That

69

whole idea fell apart because of Chinese interference. After about two months in the zone, we were transferred to another camp, a very small place called the Banana Camp because it was shaped like a banana. At last one day, the Americans drove up with a loudspeaker and announced this was our last chance. They didn't threaten us, just gave us a time limit— five minutes, I think.

We'd been prepared for something like that. We were not to listen to this because once you started listening, once you started thinking about it, you were on the point of wavering or thinking about returning. For me, not only would it have been going back on my word to the group, it was a personal decision I had made and it would have been going back on my own word—to myself.

The Americans waited around for five minutes. When no one came to them, they took down their loudspeaker and left.

Now there was terrible dissension in the group. We were sick and tired of living with each other and we were not under such strict control. When Batchelor left, that had sort of broken the group. It was unthinkable that the group leader would leave. He had always been the most trusted one and had tried hardest to keep the group together. We felt more sad than angry. Everyone liked him, and we expected that he would be sent to prison, as he was.

We woke one morning and the gates were open, and there was not a soul in sight. The Indian soldiers had left. The Chinese moved in. The commander came over from the hospital. We stayed in camp a few days and two procommunist correspondents Alan Winnington and Wilfred Burchett interviewed us. The Chinese agreed to a general press conference at Panmunjom, and we spent several days training for that— possible questions and how to answer them. We were to stress the McCarthy theme and imperialism and peace. Corden was now the group leader. He was twenty-five. He had been in the Army since 1946 and had the highest I.Q. of all those who went to China. He made a long speech and then we all answered questions. They were pretty much what we had expected.

After that, we prepared to go to China—twenty-one Americans and the British Marine Condron. Several of the group had ideas about going to Russia, not China, but the Chinese talked with them personally and convinced them to go to China. Then Commander Tien read a little speech accepting us, as free citizens of America, for China. We signed papers saying we wanted to go to China. And we had a party, and we and the Chinese all got very drunk.

We spent a few days in Kaesong, having civilian clothes made, walking around the city and taking excursions. They had a special train made for us—an engine, a dining car, two coaches and two flatcars for our Russian-made Jeeps. We traveled through Korea, saw the devastation at Pyongyang, where there was nothing left standing and people were living in caves. Chinese photographers came aboard and took pictures of us. And about four o'clock on the morning of February 24, 1954, we crossed over the Yalu River into China. I looked out of the window; it was misty and cold—very dark, very gray, very cold.

VI

SELF-CRITICISM

It took a long time, but the moment I entered China was the beginning of my return. At that time I considered myself someone who had joined the ranks of the socialist countries. I wanted to do whatever I could to help the Chinese build up their country and develop it into socialism. I felt the United States was corrupt, that the Government was influenced, indirectly at least, by the very rich. I believed that the U.S. was imperialistic, that she was predatory in relation to smaller countries, that she was responsible for all the wars, and that the Russians were the only ones truly trying for peace. I considered myself a peace fighter. I wanted to work for peace and for the development of communism in the world. I was against war, all war, and I wanted peace. I felt more or less what the Chinese had taught me. I was gullible.

This was the peak of my development toward communism. After I entered China, my faith started downhill immediately. I wasn't self-disciplined enough to believe everything. I would think things over. I never did believe that the South Koreans started the war. If they had, why did they get pushed back to Pusan in a matter of days? Things like that kept me from going completely 100 percent communist. I discovered that so much of what I had been told about China was built on a foundation of sand that gradually, bit by bit, sifted away.

And once we reached China, we became a liability, a prob-

72

lem. We'd been used and were being gradually discarded. I felt this and events proved it to me. This started working on me.

But as our special train rumbled onto the bridge across the Yalu, I did not yet know this. The train stopped halfway across the bridge, and we sat there for about half an hour. We were told there would be a reception committee on the other side at Antung. They were probably getting everything ready. Finally, we went on into the city and got off. They had big limousines and took us to a beautiful restaurant and gave us a Western-style breakfast—scrambled eggs and bacon and coffee. The officials of the city welcomed us to China and then we were put back on our train.

It took us about a week to get from the border to our destination, Taiyüan, the capital of Shansi Province; we were sidetracked a lot to let other trains through. We spent most of the time looking out the windows, playing cards or chess; and every time the train stopped, we'd get off and wander around. Everything was so new and so strange. The Chinese gave us each the equivalent of about ten U.S. dollars in *yuan* and we bought candy and things at towns along the way. That was our first Chinese money.

On the train one evening, everyone was lying around reading, resting, talking and I remember Cowart [ex-Cpl. William A. Cowart of Dalton, Georgia] was lying in his upper berth. Just underneath, Commander Tien was sitting and talking to a couple GI's. We had been warned not to smoke in the bunks for fear of starting a fire, but Cowart was smoking and when he got through, he flung the cigarette under his bed at the open window. The cigarette landed right on Commander Tien's bald head. It burned him. He jumped up and hit his head on the bottom of the upper bunk. It knocked him back down in the seat again. He lost his glasses and he lost his temper. That was the first and only time I ever saw him lose his temper. He blasted Cowart something terrible in Chinese. He was so angry he completely lost his poise. All of us

73

were trying to laugh and not laugh at the same time, but we joked about it all the rest of the way to Taiyüan. The commander got over it, but he never forgave Cowart.

We reached Taiyüan early one morning. It was as though we had entered the U.S. at New York and been sent to a city in Wyoming. It had just snowed an inch or two, and on top of the snow was a thin film of dust. It gave the city a very dirty look. Taiyüan has a miserable climate, and because you are close to the desert, terrible dust storms. Even with all the windows shut, everything gets covered with dust. You can't keep anything clean. It's very barren country, nothing green. It was a miserable place to live, a filthy place. I came to hate it.

A bus took us to a walled-in courtyard surrounded by gray brick buildings. Our rooms were large and there were two or three men to a room. We were taken to a luncheon in our honor given by city officials and some army officers. A very nice banquet hall with tables all laid out and choice Chinese dishes and wines and Russian vodka—in those days. There was toasting and speeches about how the Chinese were proud of us for refusing repatriation and coming to China to help them build socialism. When you've heard one, you've heard them all. Then the banquet started. We hadn't really learned what Chinese banquets were like. So we gorged ourselves and were full by the fifth or sixth course, with still ten or more to come. Course after course came on, and no one could touch them. After starving for three years, this seemed a terrible waste.

We had no idea why we were in Taiyüan, but everything was still so new, it didn't matter. We were just there. And we were a liability for the Chinese; they really didn't know what to do with us.

They gave us physical checkups. My only trouble was my teeth and they found that I had high blood pressure, as I had even before I joined the Army. They tried to cure it with some

74

new Russian method which was very painful, but it didn't seem to do any good and they gave up. I still have high blood pressure.

They discovered that Sullivan had a bad case of TB and he was rushed off to a sanitarium. They cured him and he came back in about three months. They also found that Douglas [ex-Cpl. Rufus E. Douglas of Texon, Texas] had a heart defect caused by a disease he contracted in Japan. There hadn't been any treatment in the POW camp, and he had been very sick in the neutral zone. In Taiyüan, he went to the hospital and after a few weeks he got worse and died there on June 8, 1954. He was a very tall, big fellow and had been an orphan for a long time. His death shook up a few of us. He was young, about twenty-seven, and it sort of made you realize that you weren't so secure after all. Anything could happen.

The Chinese insisted on having a Christian funeral for Douglas. That was ironical because we all considered ourselves rather Marxist in those days and we couldn't understand why the Chinese insisted on a Christian funeral. They had a Chinese minister come and he read passages from the Bible in Chinese. Douglas is buried now in a cemetery outside Taiyüan.

We lived in Taiyüan from February to October. They didn't want to put us in Peking, because there were diplomats there. We were just to disappear. They didn't want any foreigners approaching us.

Taiyüan was primitive and the people were tough. It was one of the last places that had been taken over by the Communists. The people acted as if they had never seen a foreigner. The first time we went out, on our first Sunday there, three of us were followed by a huge crowd, mostly peasants in from the countryside. We headed for the center of the city and fled into a department store. The mob crashed in right behind us. They broke windows and glass cases. Finally, the manager dragged us upstairs and put us in a little room, and we had to stay there about an hour until the crowd dispersed. They had just never seen foreigners.

About two weeks later, Clarence Adams [of Memphis], who is a Negro, and Wilson [ex-Cpl. Aaron P. Wilson of Urania, Louisiana] and I went walking one evening after supper. We walked to the square. There was a stand where a policeman directs traffic, although there wasn't any traffic. A Chinese fellow came, circled around us and kicked Adams as hard as he could in the seat of the pants and started shouting. He must have been cursing. He was pointing at Adams and shaking his fist. A crowd started gathering. The policeman just stood there looking. We finally got hold of Adams—who wanted to fight—dragged him away and fled back to our dormitory.

We all underwent a complete course of ideological purification the whole time from February to October. The army carried out this thought reform to get us thinking the way the Chinese think.

First, we had to attend series of lectures—the history of the Communist Party in China, communist social development. Alan Winnington, the procommunist journalist, gave us a talk on Vietnam—this was when the French were there. A Chinese military officer also talked about Vietnam: that it was a war of liberation and was going to spread throughout Southeast Asia and that China was helping the Vietnamese and would continue to help them. And even if the U.S. imperialists stepped in, they were bound to be defeated. At that time, I thought America should not come into Southeast Asia because I believed it was a genuine struggle for liberation on the part of the people there. I more or less believed then what the American university students who later were protesting the U.S. war in Vietnam believed.

After each lecture series, we had discussions and we had to relate the lectures to our own experiences. Why we had fought in an imperialist army, for example. I more or less believed what the Chinese believed: that the U.S. was rich and powerful and that she was run by the rich and it was in their interest to control as much of the world as possible. I believed that then. But I didn't consider that my life had been extremely poor; I remembered that in and around Fort Ann there had been many people much poorer than we were. But I did have the feeling that there were very, very rich people who had anything they wanted, and wasted more than I would ever get in my lifetime. Before I was a POW, I had an idea, more or less like everyone else I knew, that there was this filthy-rich class of people, but then I didn't link them up with the Government in any way. That came later.

Our last course of lectures—on social development—was to prepare us for the next phase, the beginning of a very concentrated ruthless program of criticism-and-self-criticism. We were taught that man is a social animal, that the system of Karl Marx and Engels keeps relations between man and man as harmonious as possible, and that this system is based on the principle of criticizing others when they are wrong and being able to accept the criticism of others. This is the central idea that keeps Communist China together.

This criticism system is nothing they can throw a man into right off; he would reject it. You have to learn to accept it bit by bit. When you think you are a Communist, then you automatically want to accept it. You want to put the collective interests, no matter how minor, before your own self, absolutely and totally. You must do this or you may not be a Communist; it's your duty to do it.

In Korea—and in Vietnam also—it was common to see what we would call fanatical acts and to accuse the communist soldiers of being doped. That's all nonsense. They weren't doped at all. The drug is this idea, this sense of duty. It makes them fanatical. They are very highly disciplined. To them, this sense of duty to the group is a religion.

These criticism meetings are the glue that binds Communist China together. It is the core of thought reform. Everyone in China must belong to some organization and through that organization to what is formally called a Small Study Group. This is where they go through the process of criticism-and-self-criticism. Even the top people have their criticism meetings. One or two leaders have been criticized for drinking. And I know that Ch'en Yi, the foreign minister, was criticized a number of times for wearing dark glasses and well-cut Western suits. That's one of his vices. The criticism-meeting technique controls everyone.

Everyone knows that he has to go through this criticism process. You know it is coming. It is inevitable. It is like waiting for some great punishment.

For days before a criticism campaign begins, you become very humble. You try to be as nice as you can to everybody else. Everyone is doing that. You go into the meeting shaking inside. You feel great tension, anxiety. Everyone sits around a long table. You have to face each other. And at the end of the table sits the Party Secretary with an interpreter. Everyone is in a state of half terror. Your only hope is that it won't last long.

During the periods when such a campaign is on, each small group gets together every day. You sit there from morning till night. Every member of every group must confess his sins and every member must criticize every other member. You write your autobiography—ten, fifteen, twenty pages—and read it to the rest of the group. They comment on it. You have to write it again and explain your views that the group has criticized. You read it again to the group, and they all take turns criticizing you, blasting you. Then they give you another chance to accuse yourself again—give you time to write it up again, to think it over.

You can't walk out. You go through this over and over until the group, or the Party anyhow, thinks you are really sincere about it, that you really regret having these views—that you really feel you have been wrong and will be able to correct yourself. You must repent.

And you have to criticize everyone—for something. You cannot remain silent. You have to speak against the others. You can't just sit there. When it's your turn, you've got to say something. If you fail to criticize a person, they will blast you for that. They will charge you with protecting the other person's bad side. That makes you a criminal. You have to say something against each person in your group. Sometimes you have to reach to find something to criticize. You search your memory for some little thing, any little thing, that he said that you can talk about. You have to blow it up completely out of proportion. Or you have to say he did something with the wrong motive. You are not free to remain silent. The system destroys silence.

It is absolutely impossible to keep a close friend who will hold a confidence under this system. After you have been through a number of these meetings, you are in such a state that you don't dare say anything, to anyone, that might be used against you in the next meeting. Among the Chinese, sons denounce fathers, daughters their mothers. There is no safety outside the system. Your ties to other people break.

This system has led a lot of Chinese to commit suicide. My wife's grandmother hung herself.

Some people will say, "I would not have done this or that; I would have told them to go to hell." But there is no escape. You would be assigned to digging ditches, and you would still have these meetings there. And if you fought back there, you would be sent to a camp or finally to the mines. And even in the mines you would have to go through these meetings.

Of course, over the years the Chinese have learned how to go through this process as best they can. The Chinese are like willow trees, they learn to live with life. But in those days, people really did feel honest about it. And we didn't know about the game of making yourself look black enough so you wouldn't have to go through it again.

The system deeply affected relations within our group. For example, the Southerners and Negroes got along all right, but in criticism meetings, sometimes, the Negroes would take on the Southern white fellows and attack them and question their sincerity on racial attitudes. The whites had to be humble and take it. If they resented it, they didn't show it because there was the next criticism in front of them, waiting.

I was always attacked for having a peasant mentality that says, "A bird in the hand is worth two in the bush." That was not a revolutionary worker's mentality. I was backward. I should not be so conservative. Be revolutionary. Try for two birds in the bush.

I was attacked by all the others. They attacked me one after another. It is a terrible experience. Can you imagine sitting there and having every one of your best friends attacking you, blasting you, and going on like that for two and three days?

Your first reaction is to feel very, very small. You crawl. Because I'm rather honest, I thought they meant it. It made me feel sorry that I had caused them to feel this way. It was my fault. I really felt that. This continuous barrage of accusations makes you feel the whole thing is true; they can't all be wrong. All along you are saying that you will try to improve yourself, that you will try harder next time.

That's the first stage. Then, after a day or a day and a half, you get angry. You are belligerent; you don't care. You pretend you are not even listening to them, but of course you are, all the time. They can see you are getting angry, and then they have to attack you more. They beat this anger right down into you. By the end of the third day, you become like a whipped dog. You don't deserve to live. You feel you should be shot. You don't even want to look at anyone; you can't look. You just sit there with your head down.

That's how you are supposed to feel. It means you are regretting your past actions. You get a sense of determination. You will strive, you will do better. That is repentance. The Party member can tell when you have reached this stage.

Then he will sum up things and say that you realize your mistakes now and you will improve yourself.

I would repent and express my desire to try and overcome this conservative mentality and strive for a revolutionary worker's mentality. The Chinese said if there was an attempt to take over the country where I was living, I should not worry about the family or my relatives or my possessions. I should join. This is one thing I was repeatedly tested on in the group meetings. I had to reassure them of my revolutionary spirit. And at the time, I really believed I would. I really felt closer to them. Man is a social animal; you've got to have somebody to cling to.

I've heard this process described as "braincoating" and that's a pretty good description. The Communists try to put a repellent layer on your mind to repel all sorts of non-Marxist ideas and temptations.

Then it's over for you, thank goodness. Once it's over, you feel better. A sense of exhilaration comes over you. You walk out feeling that you have cleansed yourself. You really feel close to them. You feel that you have been wrong. You have repented. You won't dirty yourself again.

This is a powerful system. If Communist countries—especially China—are ever able to solve their economic problems, mainly agricultural, then, by working with these methods they are already using, I don't think there's any question but that the whole system will just streak through Asia, and far, far ahead in time, probably America, too. I don't wish Communists would take over the world. It is what I fear.

VII

SPARROWS AND SARDINES

During our course of self-criticism in Taiyüan, the Chinese were deciding what they were going to do with us. They decided they would send some of us to school, some to a state farm and the rest to a paper mill. They gave us all an exam and picked us on the basis of whose command of the Chinese language was best. I was one of eleven who went to the People's University in Peking in the fall of 1954. I was pleased with my assignment.

When we arrived in Peking, we were shifted from the control of the army to the Chinese Red Cross, which would be in charge of me all the rest of my time in China. The Red Cross met us at the train station and the woman who was its president had us in for lunch. Even between organizations in China there is a problem of saving face, and in time we learned to play one organization against another—the school against the Red Cross—when we had problems or complaints.

At the People's University, we started in the preparatory department in the western suburbs. We occupied three rooms at the end of the top floor of a dormitory. We got scholarships of ninety *yuan* a month—about forty dollars—a very generous sum. There were about three hundred Chinese students. We had our own dining hall with a few Russian and Czech students. We had a Chinese janitor who brought us hot water for drinking and took care of the small coal fire we had in our room during the day because it was damned cold there in the winter. The university had about 5,000 students and more than 740 janitors.

We lived in cotton-padded clothes all the time. When we were out of bed, we couldn't take off our coats, not even to eat. It was the same in the classrooms. It would get so cold we couldn't even write.

We spent two years at the People's University. It was their highest university for political training. At first, we had preparatory classes with model peasants and model workers. They too were getting prepared to join the regular university classes. I remember one student named Kao Yu-pao who belonged to a very poor peasant family. Right after the takeover in 1949, he had written a book on peasant life that attacked the landlords and rich peasants and had a very progressive line. Some students later became members of the national legislature. And just a couple of months before I left China, I bumped into one man I had met in these classes who had risen to be a judge in the Peking Municipal Court.

Our work at the People's University was essentially language training plus political training, with a good dose of subjects on China. Maybe they hoped we would become very reliable politically and could be used in liaison with foreigners. After the first half-year, all our instruction was in Chinese. We had a course in Chinese history, courses in Marxist social development, world history, the history of the Chinese Revolution, and, of course, courses in the Chinese language all the time.

They gave to Chinese history the basic theme that the peasants have been in revolt for thousands of years, but they had failed to gain control until 1949 because of bad leadership. They taught us that only a Communist party can lead workers or peasants in their "democratic revolution" and succeed in it. That was their view and still is.

They praised the help the Russians gave China and taught us that the Chinese were following the leadership of the Russian Revolution. In those days, China was crawling with thousands of Russian technicians and engineers. Russian Communists were considered absolutely flawless, and to criticize the Russians or anything Russian was almost a crime. That's a great contrast with today's attitude.

In 1954-55, during the so-called Hu Feng movement, named after a prominent author who was under attack, we had to go through intensive self-criticism meetings all day long for two weeks or more. They were held as soon as we finished breakfast, from about 8, straight through until noon, and then from 2 until 6, and again in the evening. All classes were called off. We sat there and criticized each other; no one could remain silent. We had to write our autobiographies again and read them aloud and have them criticized.

This was a time when Chinese intellectuals were denounced by members of their family. Hu Shih, who was probably the most outstanding intellectual in modern China, was denounced by his son who had stayed on the mainland when his father went to Taiwan. It was very common for sons to accuse fathers, husbands to accuse wives.

Despite all the study and indoctrination, we did have time to relax. School normally stopped every day at 4, and everyone was required to go outside and exercise, play basketball or Ping-Pong, which the Chinese call *bing-bong chiu*. And on Saturday night there was always a dance at the school. It was all right to dance in those days, although for a couple of years before I left, it was prohibited as a foreign element. In the summertime, the dances were held outdoors. Most of the couples would be two men. It was just not proper to touch or come close to a girl. There was nothing homosexual about it; just that their puritanism was so ingrained. When a boy or girl danced together, they would usually be from Shanghai, where people seemed to be faster and looser. I didn't dance myself; I used to go to the dances to look around a bit and perhaps play Ping-Pong.

As time went on, an American couple, William Hodes and his wife, became the center of the social life of a number of foreigners. We used to go to their house frequently. A Chinese-American had a band organized and we used to make a night of it—dancing, playing poker—indulging in all the "corrupt" things the Chinese were trying to do away with.

Hodes worked for a research organization and his wife worked for the radio station. To show you how effective the Chinese indoctrination system can be, once their children walked in and demanded that we stop gambling or they would report us. That ended our poker playing at their house. But the parents were worried about what was happening to their children and they all left China about 1958. As far as our Government knew, they had only been in Russia all those years.

Some of the foreigners used to hang out at a couple of places in the center of Peking known as the Peace Café and the Black Cat. They were like coffee shops but you could get liquor there. They stayed open until twelve on Saturdays and eleven other nights. But all you had to do was to buy a supply of liquor, Chinese beer or brandy, just before closing time, and you could sit there as long as you wanted. That's what we used to do. Quite a number of White Russians would hang out there, too. Mostly only foreigners went there, and eventually there would be a brawl or two among them. Chinese girls used to hang around, and you could still pick up a girl whenever you wanted to. This is before they really clamped down. Some were dyed-in-the-wool prostitutes; others were just girls who wanted to marry a foreigner to get out.

The owner of the Peace Café was a big fat man, a Chinese, and he owned the café completely in this period, 1954. But the State started taking over private businesses and gradually took over his place. First they took half of it, then all of it. He tried hard to get out of China; he wanted to go to some foreign country. But he never managed. When I left China, he was still there, sort of retired, helping them supervise the place.

In those days, there was also a place called the Russian Club run by the Soviet Embassy for the White Russians living in Peking. There was quite a colony of White Russians in China then, but most of them were forced to move on in 1958 and afterward. Some of them had been teaching Russian, some had technical jobs, but later they could not earn a living. The Red Russians regarded them as Russians, but they regarded themselves as stateless, and most of them eventually left for South America and Australia. Most of the White Russians hated the Soviets and some of them wouldn't even go to the Embassy's Russian Club.

The bar keeper at the Russian Club was a well-known hermaphrodite. The story was told that in his early years he owned a house of prostitution that was patronized by American Marines. He was a woman in those days. When the Communists came in, they closed the place down and he—or she —went to Shanghai. When he came back from Shanghai, about the time I got to China, he was a man. An American friend of mine, who had been in China for many years, asked why he had changed his sex, and he said he was getting old now and couldn't pretend to be a woman anymore. It seems that the Chinese had put him in jail but had let him out.

One Sunday in 1955 I was going to a little village near the People's University and on the way back passed a courtyard and saw a public execution. There were two men, one had been accused of rape and the second of some other crime. The Chinese must have had a trial and gotten the men to admit their crimes. That's the Chinese way: through their process of self-criticism, the man eventually admits it. Now they were tied there, hands and feet, and blindfolded. And I saw an officer simply walk up and shoot each man through the back of the head. One time.

I found two lovely little markets in Peking, the Tung-an and the Lung-fu-ssu markets. Lung-fu-ssu is now called the Jen-min, or People's Market; if you asked for the Lung-fu-ssu market today, unless you asked a very old person, no one would know what you were talking about. In those days, the Chinese shopkeepers had their little shops all close together with aisles running through. They would sit around and talk and play Mah-Jongg. You could get almost anything; all sorts of handicrafts, old books, food, U.S. surplus materials from the Chiang Kai-shek days, paintings, antiques, everything you could imagine. I used to love to go down there and wander around all day Sunday and absorb some of the old Chinese society.

But then came the intensive movement of the State taking over private enterprise. The State took half ownership of every business. There were parades with businessmen carrying huge red banners with yellow lettering saying how glad they were to have the government as their partners. Every shop put up a huge banner, saying, "We welcome the movement to take over private enterprise." And all the little shopkeepers in my favorite markets were taken over. They had to put up little banners. But the look on their faces was a contrast. All these brightly colored banners, but they'd be sitting there with their faces a mile long. On Sunday morning I talked to a few of them. They would look around carefully and then say, "They own half of it now, and in a year, they'll own all of it." They knew the end was coming. Bit by bit, the market disintegrated.

One day in 1955, our interpreter came in and said an old friend wanted to see me in the office. I went around. There was this young Chinese in army uniform with a pistol. In those days very few Chinese carried pistols. I knew he must be from security. He said we had met in Camp 5 in Korea, but I didn't know him. He said he was now working with a secret organization and had been reading through the files and had found an autobiography I had written in the POW camp—four years earlier! We had all made up fantastic stories for those autobiographies. I had included that I had served in the Army in New Mexico, guarding military installations. Now, he wanted to know, were they nuclear installations and could I draw a diagram of them? He questioned me for an hour. I had a hell of a time convincing him that I hadn't been anywhere near there. To this day, I don't know whether he believed me or not. It was very thorough of them to go way back into those old records. And that was my first hint of the Chinese nuclear program.

During our winter vacation in January 1956, several of us were taken for two weeks on a sponsored trip to Tientsin, the port city of Peking. This was my first trip outside Peking. We enjoyed ourselves and had very good treatment. They put us up at the best hotel; all the silver was marked Astor House. It had once been British owned. We were taken to an old British club, a fabulous place, that had been turned into a workers' club. It had a racecourse, an indoor swimming pool and a huge dance floor that moved on springs. We hadn't seen anything like this in years. We went there a number of times to swim in the pool.

We took a side trip to visit the colliery in a small town near Tangshan. The train didn't go all the way so we had to wait in the freezing cold until they packed us into an old U.S. three-quarter ton truck. The drive took hours and we nearly froze. But once we got there, they had hot food waiting for us and showers, and we went to bed. The next morning they showed us around and explained that the mine used to belong to the Japanese. They quoted a lot of figures showing how they produced more coal than the Japanese.

They took us down the shaft, after outfitting us with uniforms and helmets with lights on them. They gave us our own little private train down there, one man in each car. And the last thing the mine director said, very seriously, was to be very, very careful not to lose your helmet or your light. I was in the last car and they took us right up to the face to see them ripping out the coal with automatic cutting machines. Returning to the elevator, our Chinese interpreter was sitting in the car ahead of me. The cars were bouncing along and suddenly I saw his helmet fly off. It fell between his car and mine. I made a grab for it, missed, and it fell on the track and derailed my car. I was spilled out. I rolled in the dust but didn't get hurt. The mine director came back fuming. He wanted to blow his stack but he couldn't because we were foreigners. Nothing was said, but later I heard that this interpreter, his name was Wu, really caught hell and was transferred.

Back in Tientsin, we visited Betty Chandler and her husband. He is one of China's top chest surgeons, and she is an American who had come out to China and married him. Her husband had been very rich and was still getting a fabulous salary. They lived in a wonderful, large house and he had three cars and modern appliances. He had been a landlord's son who studied medicine in America and was well established when the Communists took over. He offered his services to the Communists and was allowed to keep his wealth. Five or six years later, Betty left him and got a job in Peking at the Foreign Languages Press. It took her a long time, but she finally got a divorce from him.

We spent our second year at the People's University at a branch inside the city. We lived in an old, dark, run-down Japanese building, two people to a room. I roomed with Sullivan and we got along very well. He liked sports a lot and so did I. But he finally went to work in a factory and I moved in with Corden. He was extremely intelligent: my I.Q. was 106, but his was 142. He liked to drink, but he was a very nice guy. Later he went to a factory in Wuhan to work and then went home in 1958. He wrote me from Hong Kong.

I didn't know much about drinking. I would only go on a binge maybe twice a year. I remember one evening at the home of the journalist Alan Winnington, they had a party and put me to making punch. They figured I was the most reliable—alcoholically reliable. I didn't know the first thing about making punch so I just started pouring a little of everything into a big wooden bowl. They slopped it down, really liked it. I tried it and it tasted pretty good. So I went back and made some more, and by one or two o'clock everyone was on the floor. By four in the morning, I couldn't even move. They had to carry me back to school and put me to bed. I lay there for twenty-four hours before I could even get up. But it was seldom that I went on a spree like that.

Early in 1955, while we were at the People's University, three of our group who had been sent to the farm returned to the United States. This shook the whole group. They were the first to go back: Cowart, Lewis W. Griggs [of Jacksonville, Texas] and Otto Grayson Bell [of Lake, Mississippi]. Bell was the only one among us who was married back in the States. We saw them when they came through Peking. Some of the others might have tried to talk them out of going home; I didn't. Of course, we all thought they shouldn't be going back. To us they were committing a crime, deserting the group and deserting China, too. The difference was that in the school we had this continuous, intense psychological training; those on the farm didn't. In time, those of our group who lived like the Chinese on a farm or in a factory all found life unbearable.

We figured that those first three would be arrested and thrown into jail when they did return to the U.S. They were arrested by the U.S. Army, but the Supreme Court later ruled that the Army could not try anyone who had been discharged. Since we all had been given dishonorable discharges when we entered China, they had to release those three.

During this period, I bought a shortwave radio. Of course, an ordinary Chinese could just walk in and buy one; but I couldn't. I had to get a letter from the school and a permit from the police. I considered myself working with the Chinese cause, but I still wasn't trusted—and that hurt.

Having a radio that could pick up foreign broadcasts made me suspect to our interpreter. He seemed afraid that I would influence the ideas of others in the group. After I bought it, I was anxious, too. So I took it to a repair shop and had them fix it so I could hook on earphones and listen without anyone knowing what I was listening to. Eventually, they got used to the idea of my having a radio.

Morris R. Wills when he joined the U. S. Army at age 17.

Kai-yen, as she looked as a student when she and Wills met.

The 21 Americans and the British Marine just before entering Communist China as defectors. This picture was taken on January 26, 1954, at Panmunjom, Korea. The dog was the group's mascot. Wills is the ninth from the left in the back row.

Some of the group when they visited Peking in May, 1954. Wills is not in this picture.

Part of the group at the Wall of Nine Dragons, Peking in May, 1954. Wills is fourth from right in rear row.

The first picture Kai-yen sent to Wills after they met.

Wills towers over two People's Liberation Army basketball players at Peking University.

The Peking University basketball team in early 1957. Wills was the star of the team; their coach was American-educated.

On a taxi ride during vacation at the seashore, 1959.

Wills and Kai-yen just after their marriage in Peking, 1961.

Wills and his graduating classmates at Peking University, 1962.

Kai-yen with their baby in Peking, 1965.

Wills enjoyed his guitar and his short-wave radio at the Foreign Languages Press in Peking.

Wills carries a sign reading "Defend Freedom of the Seas" at demonstration in Peking during the Cuban missile crisis.

Wills, second from right, listens to Premier Chou En-lai, who visited Foreign Languages Press when Wills worked there.

Wills and his Russian roommate, Sasha.

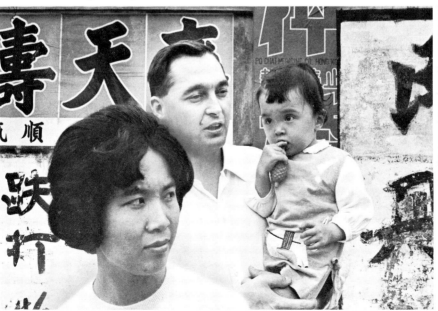

Wills and Kai-yen, carrying their baby daughter, step out of Communist China and cross the line into Hong Kong.

James Hansen photographed the Wills family in Hong Kong shortly after their return to the free world.

Wills visits his father on the family farm in West Fort
Ann, New York, after an absence of 15 years.

But in the beginning, it had been difficult. I remember that when we first arrived in Taiyüan, there was a shortwave radio in each room, and Belhomme [ex-Cpl. Albert C. Belhomme, born in Belgium] turned it on and was listening to some hot jazz on the Voice of America. There was a terrible row; some of the others shouting that this was bourgeois and he shouldn't be listening to decadent jazz. They had a criticism meeting for Belhomme. Poor Belhomme, just because he wanted to listen to American music, he had to go through the whole process and repent. And after that, no one was allowed to listen to shortwave, until I bought my radio.

By the end of our stay at the People's University, there was a lot of dissension in our group. This had been building up. We were isolated from others, and didn't have many contacts with the Chinese. We got tired of seeing those same eleven faces day in and day out. And we were sick of the intensive criticism meetings that went on all the time in our classrooms. Some—Hawkins and maybe Rush [ex-Pfc. Samuel D. Hawkins of Oklahoma City and ex-Cpl. Scott L. Rush of Marietta, Ohio]—got politically disillusioned first. One or two found themselves White Russian girl friends in town and would stay away two or three days at a time. Some got fed up with studying. We all felt we were being kept in a confined space, a closed room. We got into heated arguments frequently. Not everyone was a fine character to live with.

At the beginning of 1956, I asked the director of the college to let me leave the group and go to a factory. I wanted to get away from some of them. I wanted to get into a Chinese atmosphere so that I could integrate with the Chinese, learn Chinese properly and live at their standards. None of us had broken through this barrier with the Chinese.

The Chinese seemed glad to split up the group. Hawkins, Rush, Sullivan and Andrew Fortuna [of Greenup, Kentucky] were sent to factories in Wuhan and Peking; Clarence Adams, Corden and Webb [ex-Cpl. Harold Webb of Jacksonville, Florida] went to Wuhan University. Condron went to teach

English at the Foreign Languages Institute in Peking. They wanted me to remain in school because I was good in Chinese. I guess they still hoped to make something of me. So they asked me if I would like to go to Peking University by myself. I said all right as long as I could go by myself and get away from the group. That was a good break: Peking University is China's great university.

That summer before I was transferred, Condron, Fortuna, White [ex-Pfc. William C. White of Plumerville, Arkansas] and myself went on a trip, organized by the school, to Dairen. The Russians still had a great naval base there at that time. We stayed outside the city at a naval school for training Chinese commercial sailors. The city was full of White Russians and the street signs were printed in both Russian and Chinese. It was a very clean place.

We spent most of our time swimming from a rocky beach near the naval school, and while we swam, we watched them training parachutists to drop in the water and be rescued from the sea. We saw many Russian soldiers and sailors around there. One day our interpreter was taking pictures of us down by the seashore, and a guard walked over and demanded to see the camera. They had a big row, and finally the interpreter had to go with him. They developed the film and gave us only a few shots back. There were naval ships in the background of the others.

We stayed there almost a month and could roam freely about the place. We could walk as far as we wanted to. I even walked up to the reservoir, way back in the hills. No one was watching us. In those days the Chinese had confidence in me, and allowed me to go where few Westerners ever had been.

That fall I became the only American student in Peking University. I was the last of our group to leave the People's University, and on the Sunday afternoon before classes started, they brought a big Czech-made red university bus around and drove me to the foreign students' office at Peking

University. The university, which is the most highly respected in China and has the best faculty, is northwest of the city, almost to the edge of open farmland.

It is like driving into a lovely Chinese park. Magnificent grounds like a Chinese landscape painting. The main gate is red and the buildings have glazed tile roofs. There are long sweeping walks and many pine trees. One enters over a camel-back bridge that crosses a moat.

That evening I saw an outdoor movie and caught a terrible cold. Classes started the next day. Some foreign students were there, mostly from Eastern European countries, some Koreans, some Vietnamese, one Russian at this time. In the room next to mine was a fellow from Thailand, who had been involved in a coup in his country. I thought the other students didn't seem very socialistic. They talked rather frankly, played jazz records and horsed around. I was far more serious than any of them.

The best year was the first, 1956-57. There were no more small-group and self-criticism meetings. Everyone was friends then, among the foreigners and with the Chinese, too. The policy was to permit freer contacts between Chinese and foreigners, especially Russians. We foreign students had our own parties. I had my own corner room on the first floor of a large three-story, gray-brick building on the campus. There were only a few foreigners in that building. Most were Chinese teaching assistants and teachers. There was a bathroom for each corridor, and because foreign students were living there, they built a shower for the building. In time, I fixed up my room with Chinese paintings and simple white curtains. There were three doors to the building but only one was kept open, the one in the center. The other two were locked. At the center door was a so-called "friendly worker" who kept check on all the foreigners' comings and goings.

We ate in a dining hall for foreign students in a one-story building with a very high roof. A few Chinese professors and the dean of the school also ate there. The food was sort of

93

Western with a lot of Russian flavor. The Koreans and Vietnamese and anyone else who wanted it could get Chinese food prepared specially for them. The cooks were mostly old, large, jolly fat people who had worked for foreigners before. In fact, the cooks and the big officials are the only people in China who stayed fat even during the hard times.

Some of the classes were large, with as many as two hundred students, but usually they were very small and the professor came around to be of assistance. You could ask him questions. I wouldn't say that he knew every student but he certainly knew every foreign student personally. I had many teachers who were very, very good. One, now a trusted Party member, was trained in Germany; he's frequently sent abroad to visit foreign teachers.

Everyone knew I was an American because I was on the varsity basketball team, the only foreigner on a sports team there. I played center and was rather good. Back home in high school we had had a little club, the Future Farmers of America, and I was on their basketball team. I wasn't one of the better players then, but in China I used to average 26, 27 points, sometimes 35 or 40. I suppose I was an attraction; people used to come from miles around to see this foreigner play. This was the most enjoyable time of my stay in China. I was treated as just a person.

We played in the gymnasium a couple times each week and went into town every Saturday night and played at the Peking Municipal Gymnasium. Afterward, we would go to a little Chinese stall and have some noodles. Then we'd go to a coach's home and play Mah-Jongg. Our head coach had gone to Stanford; his name was Tung Hua-yao. We all used to go out together, and with members of the team I was treated as just one of a friendly bunch of guys. This was exceptional because to a Chinese a foreigner is someone in a completely different class that you can't and shouldn't approach. But with the team we really used to have some nice times.

The next year I was assigned a roommate. At first I objected; when you have a single room, you don't want to give it up. Anyhow he came. A huge fellow, taller and much broader than I am; he must have weighed 240 pounds. I knew him as Sasha Leztov; he was a Russian from Leningrad. He came to the university with a large group of Russians, 76 or so. Sasha was a Communist and in charge of all the Russian students in China. He was a student himself, and later studied the Tibetan language and the Chinese minority groups, such as the Mongols and Tibetans.

I had an old U.S. Navy double-decker bed and since I was there first, I took the bottom bed. I asked Sasha if he would prefer it, but he said it didn't make any difference. He loved classical music. We roomed together about a year and a half and got along well. The only thing that irritated me was that he brought a phonograph and would stay up late playing his classical records. I just lay there and suffered. I didn't care much about classical music at two o'clock in the morning.

Sasha and I talked about communism. He used to talk a lot about America and President Eisenhower. We had to speak in Chinese, and the discussions were limited by our ability. Here we were, a Russian and an American, together, communicating in Chinese. I asked myself many times why the Chinese had picked me—the only American student—to put Sasha with. I was trusted at that time, but I had this air of independence about me. They probably wanted to put someone in with me who would help me to develop along Marxist lines. He helped me understand Russia and later the break between Russia and China.

By the spring of 1958, he would take little cynical jabs at Chinese policy and later he tried consciously to win me over to the Russian side. He was very critical of the Chinese communes and the Great Leap Forward. At the same time, my Chinese friends were trying to pull me their way. All I could do was listen to both sides and say nothing.

In 1956 had come the first shocking article against the cult of the personality, some months after Khrushchev's important speech against Stalin. That shook everything in China. I had already heard about it over the Voice of America. Our interpreter showed me the first anti-personality cult article in the *People's Daily;* he seemed to realize that this applied to Chinese leaders, especially to Mao. Mao was more or less treated as a god. I attacked this—in a Marxist way: It's not very Marxist to have one leader acting as a god.

My impression in Peking was that the Sino-Soviet dispute started over an ideological point. The Chinese have never believed that communism could be successful through elections; the Russians believe otherwise. The Chinese are trying to push the rest of the world, as much as possible, to rise up and overthrow their governments to accomplish a Chinese Communist type revolution.

There were more immediate reasons also. The Russians refused to support the Chinese in getting back Quemoy and Matsu, the offshore islands still held by the Nationalists, and they refused to give them help in making their atomic bombs. When, during the hard times in 1959-61, there was rationing in China, and some starvation, the Chinese Communist Party spread the word that the Russians were partially to blame for these difficulties. This, of course, angered the Chinese people and helped make them hate the Russians.

After the Hungarian revolt in the fall of 1956, the eight or nine Hungarian students at the university became outspokenly anti-Russian—very cynical about the Russians who had suppressed the revolt ruthlessly. You could almost see their fear and anger. As time went on they used to make some of the most reactionary statements about communism. At first, I was appalled; they were supposed to be part of the socialist camp. But I suppose in the long run this helped change my views. The Hungarian students and I became good friends in the end. Some wanted to get out, to go to America; that was common among a lot of foreigners I met at Peking University.

Right after the revolt had broken out in Hungary, I got

hold of several issues of *Time* magazine and some newspapers through a Reuters correspondent. They had the whole story of the Hungarian revolt and I read them avidly. I kept them in my place, and a few Chinese came in and looked through them with interest too. I suppose word got around that I had American propaganda on the Hungarian revolt. The whole story hadn't been given to the Chinese.

One night I was in my room, and suddenly, the door was thrown open and this character was standing there, in a dark raincoat, smoking a cigarette. Even without knowing who he was, I immediately told him, you close that door and knock. He politely closed the door and knocked. So I invited him in and told him that when someone visits a foreign friend he should knock first. I asked him what he wanted, and he said he had just thought he'd come over to visit me. An absolute stranger!

I had been pecking out a letter on my typewriter, learning to type. Maybe he thought I was doing Morse code or something; maybe that's why he threw open the door unexpectedly.

He gave me a name which must have been false and said he was a third-year student in the history department. I figured he was probably a Chinese undercover agent. Immediately, he turned the subject to the Hungarian revolt, and I very blandly repeated what I had read in the magazine. I was belligerent. I didn't like the way he had entered and I didn't like the idea that I was being watched. Then he asked how I knew all that was going on. I said I've got it here in these magazines. He wanted to borrow them. I said you can keep them; I've read them. Later I regretted it.

The watershed in our lives was the Hundred Flowers Movement in May 1957, and its aftermath, the Anti-Rightist campaign. All life in China divides into "movements"; the whole thing sort of dates from one movement to another. The Chinese word is *yun-tung*.

The Hundred Flowers came at a time when the Party was

97

feeling very confident. They had had nothing but success in nearly every field. Their foreign policy was working well; their economic situation was fine. They had managed to confiscate private industry, and they'd taken over the land and that was being collectivized. They were very cocky.

So Chairman Mao thought that, for propaganda purposes, it would be fine to let everyone say what he wants because apparently everyone was happy. Mao came up with the old expression in Chinese philosophy: "Let a hundred thoughts contend, let a hundred flowers bloom." Very nice. Let everyone say what he thinks and we'll all live together.

But the Chinese were seething inside. They're like that; they'll be smiling at you, but inside they may hate you. And the way the people reacted to Mao's idea shocked the leaders so much—actually terrorized them for a time—that they thought the whole thing might collapse in revolt. From that point on, they became more and more strict, more and more rigid.

The real upsurge of the Hundred Flowers Movement began at Peking University. I first noticed a number of posters, large sheets with Chinese characters, presenting the views or slogans of some person and the person's name on it. He was advocating something. By the next morning, the university was flooded with posters. They were pasted up all over. Everyone thought the Party was honestly soliciting frank opinions from everyone. I can remember my Chinese friends coming in smiling and telling me, "Well, you see, a new atmosphere. We can say anything we want to. I'm going to criticize our Party Secretary." Several of them asked me, "What can I write? What can I criticize? I've got to say something." I would just make a joke; I didn't want to get involved.

By the third or fourth day, the posters came on like an avalanche. All the walls, outside and inside the buildings, were covered, and more posters were pasted on the roads. You had to walk on them. They were hanging on strings from one building to another. And by this time the whole thing was spreading throughout the country.

The posters started getting very nasty, very critical, ruthless. One said there were onions and poisonous weeds among the hundred flowers. Once some of these appeared, more did, very angry in tone. Then people started giving speeches, standing on chairs anyplace there was a crowd: damning Russia, damning the Korean War because of all the money that had been spent, damning Party members, professors, the Party. Some expressed favorable comments toward the United States.

All classes had stopped by this time. The school was in terrible confusion—masses of people roaming all over the campus—day and night. Foreigners were completely forgotten.

This lasted several weeks before the Party cracked down. I had been suspicious from the beginning and warned all my friends to be careful. They had laughed at me. But the Party came out with an editorial on June 8 saying that this would have to stop and calling for a counterattack. This was the great turning point.

Then the Anti-Rightist Movement replaced the Hundred Flowers. The Party said that "Rightist elements"—that's when the term was first used—were taking advantage of the relaxation, and that a number of people had been deceived by these Rightists and were attacking the Party and the government. This was something that could not be permitted and they'd have to crack down. They told everyone that now they must each write ten more posters praising the Party and the government. They attacked those whose criticism had been the harshest. The next day the walls and the whole road were pasted down again with another layer of posters.

The Party started the harshest criticism meetings. Every person had to write up in detail his activities during the past month—what he had written, what he had said, what he had heard. And each person in turn had to go through days of self-accusation and of concentrated accusations by the others.

Then the suicides started. In the university alone, the first one jumped off the top of one of the hostels; others threw themselves down wells, hung themselves. And this was going on throughout the rest of China, too. It was really hard. Being accused by your best friends, day in and day out, will drive a person to suicide.

I saw one suicide myself one evening after playing basketball. I had changed and was coming back to our dining hall. I had to pass the philosophy building and I looked up and here was this man on the third floor standing spread-eagle in the window. He shouted something and plunged out, head first. As he did, people came rushing to the window, shouting. He had jumped right in the middle of a criticism meeting. He came down head on, just like he was diving into water. I rushed over and a big crowd gathered. He had broken bones all over his body. He died in twenty minutes.

This went on for months. They examined everybody and then went back and gave the worst ones a real going over. Some of my friends were labeled as Rightists. Numerous people just disappeared overnight. A lot were sent to forced-labor camps in northeastern China. Those who hadn't been so critical stayed, but each one lived a prisoner's life in his own organization. Nobody would look at him. He had to go around with his head bowed all the time or he would get into more trouble. Everyone was afraid to talk with him. A shock went through the whole country—through everyone, including me. From then on in China, it was different.

Everything started going wrong in 1958 with the beginning of the Great Leap Forward. The Party put on pressure to increase production by mobilizing the people and creating small backyard industries throughout China. The leaders had the idea that if economics was ruled by Party fervor nothing was impossible.

At this time there was a conviction that the Chinese could

do anything. "We'll cover a thousand years of development in a hundred. We'll catch England in fifteen years." It was worked up to a higher and higher pitch each day. The atmosphere was one of madness.

The Russians had launched their Sputnik on October 4, 1957, and China's post-Sputnik isolation grew bit by bit, until now it reached almost impossible proportions. Part of the Great Leap Forward was a movement to make steel. Everybody had to make a mud furnace and then go around and pick up every scrap of steel he could find. They even went into people's houses and took their pokers and grates to melt down. They made crude iron ingots. The Peking University furnace was behind the Democracy Building where the Western languages department was located. Everybody was making steel, and when I say everybody I mean hundreds of millions of Chinese.

But everything was done in such a sloppy way that these ingots were still lying around when I left China. They were never used; they couldn't be used. Ten thousand people in the university had worked for a couple of months on this and no material good came from it.

In the summer of 1958 came the movement to set up the communes. That was frenzied too. It was a gigantic and radical attempt to combine the agricultural cooperatives into large, totally communistic communes in which all the peasants, hard-working or lazy, were paid according to their needs. Students were sent out into the countryside to help form these communes. The feeling was: "It doesn't matter how many people we've got, we can feed as many as we want to. We can feed the whole world." This movement went on and on for a whole year before it ended in disaster.

And the Chinese organized an effort to bring intellectuals and students in touch with physical work. It's hard for an American to understand, but the Chinese intellectual doesn't have the slightest idea of what physical work is like. He doesn't know what the person who does this sort of work feels.

We think nothing of mowing the lawn or fixing a bicycle, but a Chinese intellectual wouldn't have the slightest idea of how to go about it, and he wouldn't do it anyway: it's beneath him. This attitude is frowned on by the Communists but it persists.

I remember while we were still in POW camp in Korea, we had an instructor who had graduated from a university in Shanghai. One day he came around with his big metal cup that the Chinese drink tea from. He was asking everyone for hot water. We thought he wanted some to make tea, so we filled his cup with hot water, and he went away. Well, about fifteen minutes later I passed where he was sitting at a table with his cup in front of him. I walked in and asked him what he was doing. He said he was cooking an egg. I thought that was funny; he didn't have any fire. So I asked him, "Where are you cooking it?" He said, "I'm cooking it here in this cup." And he lifted the lid and I looked in, and there was this egg, lying in the bottom of the water. "How are you cooking an egg in this?" I asked him. "Well," he said, "I've got hot water and there's the egg and it's in the hot water." He really thought he was cooking that egg. It is amazing how little Chinese intellectuals could do with their hands.

Everyone was mobilized to go north of Peking to a place called the Ming Tombs and help build a huge dirt dam. Mao and Chou En-lai and the other top leaders went out. Hundreds of thousands of people camped out there and worked. After basketball practice one night, the coach and the team's political leader told us it would be nice if the team went and worked as a unit. Of course, if you weren't politically all right—too bourgeois or had a girl friend or were caught stealing or wore your hair long—you weren't allowed on the team. We all decided to go together. Actually, I had three invitations: from my Chinese class and with the foreign students, in addition to the team. I chose to be with the basketball team.

I borrowed a U.S. Army sleeping bag from Jack Dunn

[ex-Cpl. John R. Dunn of Altoona, Pennsylvania], who was recovering from an ulcer, and I wore tennis shoes and old clothes. After a long bus ride, we saw tents and huts all over the area. Each school or institute had its own area. We got up early each morning and worked as a team, some digging, some carrying—just digging it out of here and putting it over there. Hundreds of thousands of people were doing this—like a huge anthill.

We stayed at the Ming Tombs five or six days. I ate the Chinese diet and got hungry because I was used to more solid food. By the end of the week, we were filthy; there was no place to take a bath. I was getting tired and sore and a bit fed up. But there was a good atmosphere about it—of a big community effort. And it did acquaint Chinese intellectuals with what it really means to have to do that sort of work.

From time to time there were "movements" against the four pests: sparrows, flies, mosquitoes and rats. That fall came a special movement against sparrows. This was a frenzied affair. It lasted for three days. On the first day, I was sleeping peacefully at about 4 in the morning. Suddenly, all this noise—tin cans, pistols, horns, gongs, firecrackers. I looked out, and there were people everywhere, on the roofs, in the streets, on the lake in boats, in trees, making noise so the sparrows would have no place to rest and would drop dead from exhaustion. The sparrows were said to have eaten too much precious grain.

This went on until after dark. Every now and then, you'd see a parade of people with a huge rack-like affair, and there were all these dead sparrows hanging from it with great banners saying "Four hundred sparrows and this makes a total of two million killed for the country."

I didn't participate. I was trying to find some quiet so I could sleep. I never had classes before 10:30 and used to get most of my sleep in the morning; I'd go to bed very late, at 1 or 2 and sleep until 10. The sparrow hunters completely disturbed my life cycle. So I fled into town to Jack Dunn's house inside the Old Wall, hoping it would be better there. It was worse. Every rooftop had somebody on it. I had to suffer for those three whole days.

And all over China crowds of people by the hundreds of millions were getting out at 4 in the morning to start banging drums and gongs. Then they would get a poor sparrow that just couldn't flap his wings anymore and club it to death. This was being done by 750 million people. Our campus used to have some beautiful birds, but I didn't see another bird for ages after that. Not a bird. Of course, the next year the Chinese admitted privately that they lost tremendous amounts of grain to the insects which the sparrows had been eating. The sparrow campaign had disturbed the balance of nature. So they deleted sparrows from the list of four pests and substituted bedbugs.

The Chinese are probably the world's greatest noisemakers anyway. A Chinese house has a radio going full blast, a group over there playing Chinese chess, babies over here squawling away, women talking loudly. All in a tiny room, and the doors wide open, people coming and going. That's normal. When Cantonese talk with each other, they sit close together and shout. You should hear my wife and her sister when they get together. This is a real cultural difference; Westerners are usually bugged by it.

From 1957 on, the economic situation in China had deteriorated badly. You couldn't get this; you couldn't get that. It became so bad you couldn't buy shoe polish or soap if you were a Chinese. Foreigners were still able to get most things. The Chinese could get just enough to eat.

Now, in 1959, suddenly there was practically nothing to eat. The anti-sparrow campaign had seriously hurt the grain crops, and the effort to turn farms into communes had failed. I woke up one morning and discovered I couldn't buy anything. In town long lines of people waited to get just a leaf of cabbage, and the people at the end of the line got nothing.

The university was forced to set up a special store for foreign students. Most foreigners didn't suffer. I could get essentials and had enough to eat. Foreigners had their own dining hall and the Chinese were not allowed inside. Food was kept on the side for foreigners and officials, for the president of the university and the Party Secretary. They had theirs; they had no worry.

Then came rationing. Of course, just having ration tickets didn't mean that you could get something. People in the countryside flooded into the cities, thinking there were more things there. But the cities were just as bad off as the countryside. Everyone was in a terrible temper. Every time I rode on a bus, there was an argument or a fight. This was the period of hard times, '59, '60 and '61. For three years, everyone was disgusted, angry, hungry, dirty, ragged.

My Chinese friends would drop in. One would tell me all his hardships, how his children were starving, his wife emaciated. At the end of the conversation, he would ask very politely, could you buy me a can of sardines? I couldn't give things to everybody; it was impossible. But for the best of my friends I bought as much as I could get away with and gave it to them. Over three years, I bought many cartons of cigarettes and at least a thousand cans of sardines.

The old people, who were the worst off physically, started dying. And children, especially babies. It was a common thing in the countryside to find a baby lying at the side of the road —thrown away. It died and they just threw it away. One of the men from our group had an infant who died. This fellow was working in a factory in Wuhan, and his situation was as bad as the Chinese's. His child died. He told me that the child died from lack of nourishment. They just couldn't get food. The baby's death made him very bitter; he left China long before I did. And the Chinese were just as bitter when one of their children died.

VIII

KAI-YEN

I had met a number of Chinese girls and gone out with some of them, but nothing very serious. It's particularly hard for foreigners to date Chinese girls. In 1958 and '59 it could still be done if one was careful. But you certainly couldn't have an affair with a girl; she'd be sent away to a camp.

The Chinese tend to be very puritanical and they try to discourage relations between Chinese girls and foreign students. They have the idea that all foreigners just want to take a girl to bed. I remember when the first Egyptians came, right after the Suez crisis. Everyone was very friendly and one Egyptian student I knew, Abdula Abaye, eventually found himself a Chinese girl friend. They saw each other quite a bit and the Chinese officials knew about it, but because the Egyptians and Chinese were so friendly, they looked the other way. They didn't like it but they didn't interfere. Then suddenly relations between the two countries got strained and the Chinese attitude toward Egyptians changed immediately. A couple of nights later, Abdula was seeing his girl off at the bus stop and just as he left her, she was grabbed by four men and hustled off. Abdula tried everything to get her freed; the girl was pregnant with his child and he wanted to marry her. But the girl disappeared. He made such a fuss that the Chinese eventually told him he had to leave. It is all part of their basic concept: A foreigner is a foreigner and just can't be part of the clan. That plus the idea that you are not supposed to be chasing girls. It's not proper to spend a lot of money or to dress elegantly or stay out late with girls.

By the time I left China, it was impossible to date a Chinese girl. The Chinese grew more and more puritanical. For several years before I left, they even prohibited dancing because dancing is a foreign element. Instead of dancing, boys and girls would play Ping-Pong. The Chinese are the world champions at Ping-Pong; they hold all the titles. They have tens of thousands of teams playing. Anyway, this sense of puritanism has become so ingrained that it's not proper to touch or come close to a girl, and, of course, a girl is not supposed to flirt with a man.

I was feeling more and more lonely as time went on and sometime in 1959, I decided that if I were going to stay in China for any length of time—and I was still planning on staying—that it was time I thought of getting married. So I made it known that I was thinking of getting married. In China when someone wants to get married, he lets it be known among his friends and people he knows, and word gets around. There has to be a formal introduction to a girl—that's still done but, of course, it's not played up so much.

My friends introduced me to two or three Chinese girls on various occasions. I went out with several of them. Then one day I was having lunch in the foreign students' dining hall and a young Chinese friend, whom I had first met while shooting baskets, sat down beside me and, after some talk, said that he had heard that I was thinking of getting married. I said Yes, but it depended on whether I found someone who would have me. He said that his girl friend had a sister who had come from Hong Kong and was in high school about a mile from Peking University. The next day he brought a photograph of her. I said I thought she looked very nice, and so he asked for a photograph of me. He had to send her the photograph through her sister and see what she said. In a few days he told me that she had said she would like to meet me.

That Saturday he came around and told me that his girl friend and her sister were over at his place and he invited me to come over. When I arrived, I remember, a girl came to the door, and I shook hands with her and told my friend I thought she was very pretty. He explained to me that this was his girl friend; her sister was in the next room. We went in and there Li Kai-yen sat—very quiet, she would hardly say a thing, just occasionally peeking at me out of the corner of her eye.

It was up to me to keep the conversation going, but it was mostly one-sided. I was there only a couple of hours and when I left I got her address. As soon as I got back to my room, I wrote her a letter, saying that I had enjoyed our visit and asking her if she would like to visit me the following Saturday. All this had to be planned for the weekends because she was still going to high school and living at school during the week.

Almost immediately I got a letter back saying that she would be pleased to come over. So I got everything fixed up, cleaned out my bachelor's room, straightened things up. I went to a lot of trouble—flowers and all.

Saturday evening I had to wait at the gate for her and, of course, she had to sign in. Everywhere you go, whenever you go into a place, you have to sign in at the gate and give your name and address and identify yourself. We walked to my place and sat there, and I showed her my photographs and we listened to music. Then I walked her back to school and we made a date for the next day.

We fell in love and from that time on, the more we saw of each other, the more we wanted to see of each other. Soon she was coming to my place when she was supposed to be in school. She'd slip out and come over.

Kai-yen was then eighteen, graceful, innocent. She had come from Hong Kong. Her father was still there and had put her and her sister in the care of her uncle, a teacher of mathematics at the high school she was attending in Peking.

She had been born in 1942 in the country in Meihsien County in Kwangtung Province, one of the southern-most provinces, adjoining Hong Kong. Meihsien County is the place where the Hakkah national minority lives and Kai-yen is a Hakkah. They have now lost most of their national characteristics but the name still sticks.

Her father's parents had been small landlords; they rented out land to peasants and worked in the fields themselves. She told me how her grandmother used to go to the fields every day and she and her sisters and brothers, little children, went out and gathered hay or weeds all day long. Life was hard.

Her mother died only a few years after Kai-yen was born. During the Second World War, her father went to Hong Kong and later to Japan. He married again, to a teacher in Hong Kong. Kai-yen's brother and sister were taken to Hong Kong, but she was left with her grandmother on the homestead. She lived there and worked on the farm right up to the time the Communists took over.

When they took over, they organized the people with no land to "struggle," as they called it, against people with land. Their whole purpose was to get control of all the land. First, divide it up and give it to the small peasants and later on take it away from them and make it into communes.

As the first stage, the whole village would be gathered together and the Communists dragged out the landlords, one at a time, and the whole village spent days accusing them of everything—a lot of it true, but a lot of it false. Once the crowd started, it would lose its head and become a mob. Kai-yen's grandmother was already over sixty, and she had to go through this. At that time Kai-yen was about ten, and one day she and other children walked in, and there was her grandmother, hanging from a rafter. Unable to bear it any longer, she had hung herself.

As soon as the mob found out that she had hung herself, they invaded the place and walked off with everything. A relative took the children in; and after some weeks, Kai-yen's father came for her and took her to Hong Kong. She lived there with her father and went to Victoria College High School until 1958. She was sent to a Protestant church there. But the family was large and it was quite a burden to educate them all in Hong Kong. Her stepmother teaches Mandarin on the island in a public school and her father had a job in Kobe, Japan, selling pharmaceutical goods through all of Southeast Asia. So Kai-yen was sent to school in Peking. Many overseas Chinese believe, correctly, that mainland education is better than that in Hong Kong and send their children back to China for an education.

After Kai-yen and I had been seeing each other for a couple of months, her uncle finally realized she was seeing someone outside the school. Her uncle was a very serious type, very strict with those two girls. He discovered that she had been signing out of the school that she was going to his home in the city. One Sunday he called her into his home and they had a terrible row. And when she told him that it was a foreigner she was seeing, he got very angry and ordered her not to see me anymore.

By this time, I had already given her a key to my place, and she'd come in anytime she wanted to. One Sunday afternoon I came back to my room from playing basketball and there she was, sobbing away at my desk. She'd written a long letter saying this is the end and that we had to break up and her whole family was against her. I talked with her and she kept on sobbing and this went on for a couple of hours. I tried to read the letter she had written but she burnt it up. She was in a terrible state. I was getting terribly worked up too. I finally got her to say that she'd go back to school and wouldn't see me for the time being, but that she would still write to me.

I decided I had to do something. The next day I went down to the Red Cross; they were responsible for me ever since leaving Taiyüan. I told them that I intended staying in China a long time, so I wanted to get married. Now there was a girl I was in love with, I said, and we were planning on getting married when she and I graduated. I told them I didn't want any interference on the part of the organization —stay out!

There were others among the twenty-one of us who had married before this, but they had tried to do it secretly and they had all had trouble. I tried to do it openly; it still didn't work.

After a week or two, Kai-yen started coming to see me again. But her uncle knew about it and they weren't on very good terms. Now the family was against me (all except her sister)—even her brother. They told her this foreigner will never marry you and besides he won't love you and if you do get married, he'll never be satisfactory, and he was a prisoner of war and maybe a spy. Her school got hold of it and her teachers; every chance they got, they'd start in: He's an American—he may be a spy—and he's a foreigner; the whole string of these feelings.

On the sly, her uncle got together with the Red Cross, Peking University and her school. This is something I didn't find out till later. They decided that after she finished her exams in the summer of 1960, they would have her transferred—from Peking to Tientsin. The Red Cross made it possible for her to be transferred to a Red Cross medical school there that they controlled. That summer her uncle suddenly told her he had arranged for her to go to this medical school. I saw immediately what was up and went to the Red Cross and tried to get them to intervene. I didn't know they were in cahoots with her uncle. There was nothing I could do.

She had to go to Tientsin even if she didn't want to. So she went. But before she left, we arranged that she would visit me. I gave her money and told her to buy a train ticket on Saturday nights (it's only two and a half hours by train), and she could stay with a friend of mine in town, who had an extra room. That worked fine for two weekends. I lived from one weekend to the next. Then the school and the Red Cross and her uncle found out she was coming back to Peking. When she came back to me on the third weekend, the school in Tientsin decided to act on its own.

It was now October. We saw each other that Saturday evening and again on Sunday. She had to go into town to buy her ticket to go back to Tientsin that night. I gave her exactly 28 *yuan;* that's more than enough for the ticket. She left me early Sunday afternoon. When she returned, we were going to have supper, and then I would take her to the train. She never showed up.

I stayed up late into the night—didn't sleep at all—fearing more and more that something had happened to her. I sent her a telegram and asked for an immediate answer. I didn't get any. By morning, I knew that they had taken her away.

That's what they do with a girl who wants to marry a foreigner; they take her and put her in a camp. I went right down to the Red Cross—stormed in there, really mad. I had tried to get married in a decent way, openly. I had told the Red Cross I intended to get married and they had interfered. I accused them of deception, called them a pack of liars, called the police fascists. The interpreter started shouting at me. I told him to go to hell, turned around and walked out.

I went straight back and wrote a letter to the president of the Red Cross—a woman who was the Minister of Public Health—and told her I wanted to leave the country immediately. I told her the whole story and said they were nothing but liars, fascists, feudal, and that as soon as I got to Hong Kong I was going to tell the whole story. I was fighting mad. If I'd been less angry, I would have thought twice about saying those things.

The first thing Tuesday morning, I got a call asking me to come down, that they would like to talk with me. I stormed down there again, still mad. They were all very nice. I met with one of the directors and he said they would find out if Kai-yen had been arrested and where she was. I said I also wanted to send some warm things to her. It was freezing cold and she didn't have anything.

In time, they told me that she had been arrested in a Peking store for stealing money. They said she had stolen 28 *yuan* —the exact amount of money I had given her. But, they said, we won't talk about that—she'll be released in a couple of days. I said that if she's going to be released quickly, I wouldn't quibble about the rest of it. But two, three days wore on. I brought blankets and things, and they said they'd send them to her. I went down again; they said maybe another couple of days. I kept after them. Then, they suddenly said she's been sent to a place in Tientsin for correction. I knew what that meant.

Much later, I found out what had happened to her. She had been picked up as soon as she left me at Peking University. There were people waiting outside and they told her she was under arrest. They took her to a detention center in Peking and were very strict with her. They made her just sit there and not do anything and every couple of hours they'd come in and question her. This went on continuously, through the freezing cold night, too. To break her down.

Then they transferred her to a small camp outside Tientsin. The charge on paper was stealing; there was no trial. They told her the real charge was her relationship to me. In China, you are sentenced to a certain place, but there is no time limit. Even if she said she wouldn't marry me, never see me again, that was not enough. She had to repent.

I didn't know what to do. I wrote a lot of threatening letters, wrote to Chou En-lai, told him the whole story and said I'd been deceived and lied to. I wrote the head of the women's federation and other people like that. I didn't get any replies, but I know they got my letters because each time I wrote one, the Red Cross would call me down and try to pacify me. A Chinese friend of mine who worked for Chou En-lai took letters personally for me to a member of the National Peoples Congress and even to Vice-President Madame

Soong Ching Ling. I met Han Suyin, the writer, and told her the whole thing and she said she'd see people she was connected with. All this went on over two or three months.

All this time I was constantly telling everyone the story of her arrest, writing to everyone and making general trouble. I refused to go to any more classes. But by January 1961 I still hadn't made much headway. I was considering whether I should throw in the whole works and leave. Everything seemed hopeless. From this point on, I really lost my confidence in Chinese Communism. I had tried to have a proper Chinese "socialist wedding," as they call it. I had tried to follow their forms, and I'd been lied to, deceived, and she'd been arrested and thrown in jail. I was still considered "progressive," but the Chinese just don't like foreigners.

I had a terrible sense of regret that I had gotten Kai-yen into this mess. Her life was too precious to waste. Now it was my job to get her out, one way or the other. Some friends advised me to stay and try to get her out and then take her out of the country; others said I should leave, hoping that they'd let her out as soon as I left. They would come and try to persuade me to play basketball, but I wouldn't. I was becoming haggard and wasn't sleeping or eating much. It was a terrible ordeal.

In January I decided what I would do and I told the Red Cross that I would go back to school the next term, but by the time the term was over, I expected her to be out and back in Peking. They gave me an ambiguous answer; they hoped I would go back to classes and maybe the affair could be settled quietly and if she repented her crime she might get out early. So when classes started in February, I went back to school.

Kai-yen managed to smuggle out a letter with a prisoner who was being released, telling me what conditions were like. I received it in the mail. That was the first time I knew for sure where she was. I went down and told the Red Cross I knew exactly what the situation was, without saying I had gotten a letter from her. The Red Cross was shook up by this. I wrote the head of her camp a very abusive letter. And then I was amazed that they made Kai-yen write me a letter, telling me what had happened and reassuring me that she was all right. That was very unusual; I figured some big official had inquired. The rest of that spring and summer they made her write me regularly. They had changed their policy and were letting us keep in touch.

When summer came, I wrote one more letter to the Red Cross, saying: If I don't see her before the next term starts, I am not going back to school and expect to leave China within a month. I also demanded that she be sent back to Peking because this was a period of terrible food shortages and no one, under any circumstances, was allowed to move into the city. They controlled people's movements by their food ration coupon. If you don't have your ration coupon, you can't eat.

School was to resume the first of October. On September 23, they let Kai-yen out. She came to Peking. After those ten months in prison, she was not depressed but very thin and frightened, shocked that they could be so brutal just because two people were in love. She went back living with her uncle, who now started being friendly. He came out to see me and said he was sorry the whole thing had happened. I went back to school and she came out to see me two or three times a week. She wasn't in school and didn't have a job.

We decided to get married right away. On November 22, the Red Cross finally gave me the special letter that a foreigner needs to get married, and the next afternoon, we took the bus into town to the registration office. Just as we got there, I realized that in the excitement I had forgotten my registration card. So while she waited for me at her uncle's home, I rushed back in a taxi, got my card, picked her up and raced into the registration office just five minutes before they closed at six o'clock.

The office was just a hole in the wall with an old oil lamp,

I remember, and a couple of little, old officials sitting around doing nothing in this dim light. When a foreigner walked in, they were all astonished. I don't suppose a foreigner had ever been in there before. We said we wanted to get married. They looked at my letter, and one man told us to wait, and I know he went out to call the Red Cross. He came back and wrote out the forms with a brush, stamped and sealed them, sort of mumbled to Kai-yen and never spoke to me. Then he asked for the fee—about ten cents in U.S. money—and shook our hands. We were married.

In China after a couple gets married, someone organizes a party and invites the friends of the bride and groom. It's a big affair and this is a Chinese, not a foreign custom. There is nothing religious about it, no ceremony. Just a lot of toasting and the bride and bridegroom tell how they met. It's all done in fun.

We had such a party. Ironically, it was organized by the Red Cross. They organized a huge affair with some thirty-six guests at the Hsin Chiao Hotel. From our group there were Clarence Adams, William White and maybe one or two others. There was dancing, even though, by now, all dancing was prohibited in China. We had a good time.

Unlike the Red Cross, the university was not reconciled to our marriage. By this time it was getting so that unless a Chinese was officially authorized, he or she couldn't come into the buildings where the foreign students lived. When I asked the school for permission for my wife to stay with me, they refused. Even though a Hungarian student was living there with his Chinese wife, the school authorities insisted that there was a rule that no Chinese were allowed to live in the same building where the foreign students were. It was irritating. So we continued to live at a friend's house.

Every foreigner in China was watched carefully by a "baby-sitter." The Chinese assign someone to meet a foreigner accidentally, become his friend and then make a habit of going to see him. Foreigners aren't supposed to know this, but, of course, old foreign residents know how it works.

My baby-sitter was in addition to the customary "foreign student's assistant"—a politically very reliable person, either Communist Party or Youth League member—who also watches you. Right after Kai-yen had been taken away, I met a Chinese fellow known to me as Lo, who was teaching sports at the People's University. He was my new baby-sitter and started coming to see me constantly, trying to calm me, telling me to take it easy and in a matter of months she'd be out. Because foreigners learn to be suspicious whenever they meet anybody new, I was careful, and in three or four weeks I knew what his real purpose was.

Lo was a nice fellow. He was big and strong, rather talkative with a good sense of humor and even liked to play practical jokes on occasion. In many ways he was a typical young Party cadre, willing to use any means to reach any end he thought was good, but he also had a strong sense of loyalty. I grew to like him and I also learned how to utilize him. If there was anything I needed, I'd just complain, and in a few days he'd walk in with it. Of course, I acted astonished, but I knew all the time he would be coming. I'd say, "Well, where did you get that? You sure do know where to get things; you know your way around." And I began to help him because the economic situation was very bad then. I used to buy him cans of meat and a lot of canned sardines and cigarettes. He could smuggle them out. And as times got harder, the things I was buying for him were keeping him alive. A bond grew between us. I suspect that in his reports he made me sound as nice as he could. Our relations became so close and he grew to depend on me so much that I probably corrupted him. He did things he shouldn't have and finally was caught and punished.

In the summer of 1965, shortly before I left China, Lo was arrested briefly—apparently for being mixed up in the black market with some other foreigners who were bringing in goods from Hong Kong through their embassies.

In the summer I would swim at the Summer Palace, a huge playground that the Empress Dowager, one of the last rulers of the Manchu Dynasty, had built with a large lake dug out by coolies with shovels. The Summer Palace is crowded and the water is dirty, and most foreigners looked down on it. I was one of the few who would swim with the Chinese.

One day when I was swimming there—and I knew that police undercover agents were keeping an eye on me—suddenly, I heard Lo summoned over the loudspeaker. He was referred to as a member of the Peking security bureau. I was dumbfounded. I didn't know whether Lo was really a security man now. I didn't know whether they were just trying to scare me. I didn't even know whether he was still in jail or not. The announcement made me wonder if he was actually a member of the police. The fact that he was identified in that way might mean that he was not. It left a hundred questions in my mind about him. Peking is really like this. China is like this. You are never really sure of anything or anybody.

Anyway, after Kai-yen had come back and we were married and living with a friend of mine, my baby-sitter popped in one day and said he had a place in town and we could live there, since he was living at the People's University. He told me not to worry about the police. Obviously, he had been told to do this. One night he took us down to his place—two rooms in a regular Chinese courtyard. We lived there for the next month or two. It was cold and hard living there but at least we had a place.

The authorities officially had not given us a place to stay, but we were being taken care of unofficially. Every little thing in a person's life in Peking is involved in this sort of thing. Once you learn to play the game, life becomes much easier.

One night in our unofficial home, Kai-yen and I were almost gassed from our little stove. In Peking many people die from coal gas every winter. I complained about our accident, and the next day the Red Cross official casually said I should try staying in the university again. So when my wife came to visit me in my room, the man at the gate told her to go in without signing in. But we still didn't quite dare to stay there. The next day, when again she didn't have to sign in, we decided to try it. No one said a word. They had made another little arrangement, all on the sly, never directly telling me anything. No one had to back down; there was no confrontation; no one lost face, and we started living at the university.

Kai-yen and I talked it over and decided that she should not go to school or take a job. I now had a long-range idea of getting out of China; the idea of leaving was already there, but I didn't have the plans or the money. At this time I was receiving a stipend of 100 *yuan* a month, about 40 or 50 dollars, but we had no rent to pay and were given furnishings, so our expenses came to only half the stipend. We figured that when it did come time to leave, if Kai-yen was working, it would be much harder for her to detach herself. As long as she wasn't connected with any organization, all I had to say was that we wanted to leave—and then leave. After all Kai-yen and I had gone through, I knew now it was only a matter of time before I would come back home to America.

IX

DISILLUSION

When I went to China, I had a vision of everyone there being completely, absolutely equal—which was one of the first things I discovered was not true. I had believed their propaganda that everyone lived in fairly decent homes, had decent clothing and food, that health was no problem and there was no crime. I was terribly idealistic at that time: It was Utopia, not from the point of view of material things but from the point of view of relations between man and man. I felt I was part of the revolution and I wanted to help as much as possible and to educate myself along these lines.

In China you grow to rely on this thing that's feeding you and maintaining you. That's the way it is throughout China now. No matter who you are or what your position is, at least you have some security. You don't have to worry about it. Once a man begins to rely on something, he becomes dependent on it and it's extremely hard to tear away from it—even if you don't like the environment.

You learn to put the collective interests, all of them, no matter how minor, totally before yourself. In America, a wrong to one man is just as bad as a wrong to five or ten. But with the Communists, wronging ten men is far worse than wronging one. A wrong to one man can be completely overlooked when the interest of two or three is involved. This idea develops to the stage of a religion; it becomes fanatic.

Until about 1958—the period of the Great Leap Forward

and the creation of the communes and the beginning of the Sino-Soviet split—I had become more and more integrated into Chinese society. After '59 or '60 I was certainly unsympathetic, but I would not say I was anticommunist yet. The longer foreign students lived in Peking University, the more anticommunist they became. Even the fanatics, in time, became almost fanatically anticommunist. The reasons: not being able to associate with the Chinese on an equal, friendly basis; always having "baby-sitters" around watching; all the daily irritations. A lot of the irritations are the result of inefficiency, but when the Chinese grow to dislike a foreigner, then it's done purposely. Some foreign students I knew wanted to go to America; I knew three from communist countries who did escape; two are now living in the United States and the third in Canada.

After 1958, the Chinese became more and more restrictive, more antiforeign. There was a strenuous effort to isolate foreigners. Any foreigner who wasn't married to a Chinese was completely cut off. I felt this even though I still had some Chinese friends, and being married to a Chinese girl opened some doors. I was able to maintain Chinese friends throughout my stay in China, but I wouldn't go to a Chinese friend's house unless it was very late at night and I was dressed up in a long Chinese coat and put on a Chinese hat and a Chinese face mask, like nurses use in hospitals here.

From one Chinese friend who worked in Chou En-lai's own complex of offices, I used to hear what the Chinese were thinking and about the leaders' private activities. He was a brilliant young man and through him I learned many things. To visit him, I would put on my Chinese tunic and face mask and borrow a bicycle. Then I could go unnoticed.

I continued to make Chinese friends—real friends. The basic reason was that my ability to speak Chinese was improving and this allowed me to circulate more freely. Of course, out of ten Chinese, maybe only two would continue to associate with you. They would be the most daring. And they tended to trust me because I was an American. They had less fear that I would turn them in. That's why, I suppose, all sorts of people came to me with their problems and their confidences. Those who would report on me, I would not cut off. That sort of person I learned to use and to give him views I wanted to reach responsible people. He could be useful.

Even though it became impossible for a Chinese to visit most foreigners, Kai-yen's relatives were allowed to come and see us and so were any of my friends who wanted to see me. When they got to the gate, they signed in to see my wife. That was perfectly all right with the Chinese.

As difficult as things were becoming for me, other members of our group had become disillusioned even earlier. In 1957 I was able to visit some of the others during my summer vacation. They were in Tsinan in Shantung Province working in a paper mill. I had made arrangements with Howard Adams [ex-Cpl. Howard G. Adams of Corsicana, Texas] to stay with him, and he showed me the city and took me through the factory. Most of the Americans there were married by then, and Tenneson, Wilson and Pate [ex-Pfc. Arlie H. Pate of Herrin, Illinois] had already left China.

The situation of those who remained wasn't very good because they had been given over to this factory to look after them and the Red Cross had washed its hands of them. Tsinan was remote and primitive. It's scorching hot in the summer and floods every year. The people were filthy and ragged and very rough. The Americans did their eight hours of drudgery each day at the factory and rode back home by bicycle. Supper was whatever their wives could throw together. Then they would lie around with their ears glued to the Voice of America—it was the only thing they had from the outside world. Maybe they would buy a bottle of Chinese spirits and drink themselves into a stupor. And to bed. The next day was the same thing.

They wanted more food and more money and better housing, but their requests were either put off or refused. They wanted to leave that place and go somewhere else, mainly to Peking. They questioned me about my situation in Peking, which was much better than theirs. So immediately after I left, the thing blew up. They went on strike, got into fights. One or two were thrown into jail by the police because the Party Secretary said they had to be intimidated a bit, so throw them in jail.

Their situation got harder. Their wives were called in and threatened. Two or three of the men were thrown into jail again because they said they wanted to leave China and go home.

In the beginning, the Chinese policy was not to let anyone leave. The Chinese told them they couldn't leave and cut off all their contact with Peking, so they could not even get in touch with the British Chargé d'Affaires. The more demanding they became, the more obstinate the Chinese became. Both sides got to the breaking point and the Chinese put several of them in jail, one after another, on various charges. They were kept in jail several months at a time, and every time they got out, they'd get into fights. Lowell Skinner [of Akron, Ohio] even punched the Party Secretary in the nose and got into a fight with the police commissioner.

All except one of them was in jail at one time or another. They wanted to get out of the place. And of those who had been on the state farm, I understand that two or three of them had been held in jail for a few days before leaving China. They had gotten fed up and bored. When they asked permission to leave and were refused, they decided to walk out of China. They walked for many miles and were picked up by the Red Army and thrown into jail and finally taken back to the farm.

At Tsinan, Howard Adams and Skinner were in jail for a good length of time. The Chinese especially wanted to get rid of Skinner because he was causing so much trouble. To do it, they talked his wife into saying that she would stay behind and Skinner could go ahead. The Chinese promised to give her a living, which they didn't live up to. When I left China, she was in Tsinan in very bad straits, barely existing. She's crippled and can hardly walk. She's a Christian. She has no way of getting out. It takes a lot of money and Skinner, as far as I know, hadn't been in a position to send for her.

I stayed in the university until the summer of 1962. During the last term more and more problems were coming along. For most of the time, we were forced to live outside and I did very little studying. Long before I completed the course, I asked the Red Cross to arrange a job for me. And in June, they arranged for me to go to work for the Foreign Languages Press, the main organization for external propaganda. I was given a two-year contract and the job of translating, proofreading and polishing copy for the English edition of the *China Pictorial*, which is a flashy picture magazine published monthly in nineteen languages. Articles came in Chinese and I had to translate them into English. Clarence Adams also worked at the Press, but as a translator in the book department.

At the Press, we were put on rations. Times were still very hard. As a foreigner, my rations were better than the Chinese had—including my wife, whose rations were average for a Chinese. For example, I was allowed four pounds of meat a month; Kai-yen's ration was two ounces a month. I was allowed about three pounds of cooking oil a month; she was allowed three ounces. I was allowed forty pounds of rice; she got twenty-six pounds a month. I was allowed thirty pounds of vegetables a month; she got only what she could buy outside and if she was able to find five pounds a month, she was lucky. But what we had together was enough to keep us going.

The Press supplied us with a two-room apartment with a bath and a small kitchen. Including water and electricity, this cost me about five U.S. dollars a month. I started out earning 150 *yuan* a month and we managed to get by. For a while we even had a maid who cooked and cleaned and did the shopping, too. We paid her 40 *yuan* a month, 20 dollars, for a six-day week, from 8 in the morning, with a break after lunch, through supper.

My work at the Press was not terribly hard but a lot of it was interesting, and our lives began to fit into a pattern there. I would get up about 7 and have a snack for breakfast, perhaps an egg and toast and instant coffee from Hong Kong, which I managed to get. At 7:30 I would listen to the radio news from Manila and from the Voice of America while getting ready. I wore just a shirt and trousers to work, very informal. At 8 I would walk across the yard and up three flights to the office. I'd read the paper and get to work. I had only about ten or fifteen days of work a month. There are just too many people in China to keep everyone busy full-time. Then I'd go home for lunch, usually rice and a couple of side dishes. We were allowed a half hour for lunch and an hour and a half for a nap, but I'd listen to the news broadcasts again and read until 2. Then back to work until 6.

In the evening most of the time, visitors would come by, mostly Chinese, and we would exchange rumor and gossip. I'd know the world's news better than anyone around there. Or we might go downstairs and play bridge with the Yangs until one or two in the morning. As we played, we would drink *maotai*, a very strong, clear white liquor. The Chinese don't get drunk, but they do get high, and we would end up playing pretty daring bridge. Then home and to bed.

Saturday night we might take the Press bus to the movies if there was a good picture playing. For foreigners they had pictures from Japan, the Soviet Union, various parts of Europe and even England, but not from the United States. On Sunday I might go into Peking and wander through the book shops or the markets or visit friends in the embassies, make a day of it. It was a rather quiet life.

The Foreign Languages Press has two thousand people working for it, including over a hundred foreigners. It is located in the western suburbs, housed in a huge building just outside the west wall. Behind it are three large housing blocks. In one live foreigners, old residents mainly, and directors of the press. We lived there. In the other two live single men and women who work for the Press. But there are not enough apartments for all of them.

The Press puts out many publications and pamphlets. There is even a secret department that translates into other languages material about China that the Central Committee wants to appear in the West, and then sends it abroad to be published in other countries. The Press is under the Propaganda Department and the State Council, which was directly under the control of Premier Chou En-lai. It is for external propaganda but also gathers information from American magazines and papers.

As the Press grew, its directors asked various communist parties to send people. They came from the British, French and German parties, among others. Most communist parties sided with the Soviet Union after the split, so the Chinese considered all these people "revisionists." That meant they were unreliable. I know several who were forced out.

The Chinese changed their policy and started getting in young university graduates, many of whom were not Communists; they were "experts"—technicians—rather than ideologists. When I worked there, that was the policy: to get people who didn't care politically. Many of the British had been helped by Dr. Joseph Needham of Cambridge University. Approaches to the States had to be done through England where it was not illegal. A couple of years before I left, they sent Israel Epstein there to recruit people in England. Most of the people the Chinese recruited recently were young, in their twenties and thirties. Most of them were given two-year contracts, and if they didn't cause any trouble, they would be offered another. It became purely a business proposition.

At the Press, I was always getting in trouble because of this same contradiction between the ideologist and the expert, the party and the professional—between the people who are politically in charge and the people who are competent and know how to do the job.

Frequently, I would get some silly thing written up in Chinese. In Chinese it might sound all right, and I, as the translator, had to stick rigidly to the text. I would not be allowed to make additions or leave omissions on my own. So when I got it translated into English, it sounded like a child had written it, full of slogans, dates omitted, figures given as "about a hundred or about two hundred," even "about two people." It was ridiculous.

Repeatedly, I would take the copy over to the Party leader of our section and say, "Now look here. It sounds like a two-year-old wrote it. Can't we change this, strike out that, get a figure here? Why don't you take this down to the editors and make these changes and reorganize the article?"

He would say to me, "If I go down there, you know how it's going to come back. Go ahead and translate it." So I'd translate it and then point all those things out to him again. Then we'd argue. I'd say, "It might be all right for a Chinese, but a foreigner wouldn't read this sort of trash. Foreigners don't speak this way, and that's who it was written for." The whole object was to get mass readership.

Sometimes I'd finally convince him to go down. He'd take the copy down and argue for maybe an hour or more. He was technically competent; he knew it didn't read well. None of the editors knew English. Then he would come back, fuming, throw the article down and say, "Of course, they won't agree with any changes." He grew increasingly angry with me for pushing him to go down in the first place.

One job I had in 1964 was to translate what was supposedly the diary of Lei Feng. He was a corporal in the army whose truck hit a telephone pole and the pole struck him on the head and killed him. The Communists had decided to make a hero of him. They wanted a peacetime hero, a symbol of the good young progressive, the Boy Scout type. Later, all small study groups had to discuss his diary. Plays were written about him, statues were built to him as the movement was built up. The campaign went on for months.

I had to translate his diary three times before they finally decided how they wanted to write it. They brought the first version to me, all very nicely made up with ten Chinese characters to a line. It took me a long time because it was difficult, with bits of poetry in it. When I finished, they told me to hang on to it; they weren't quite sure about it yet. A couple of days later, they came up with eight or nine sheets more and said they had made some changes in the diary. They had made some astounding changes. So I did it again. About a week later they came back with the final version of the diary. So I did it a third time.

By now they had made the story extremely glorious. It told how his mother had been beaten by the Japanese and he had grown up an orphan. He was supposed to be an absolute believer in Mao and studied Mao's works every day. He was said to have taken time out to help others, and teach them Mao's works. He was an example for all Chinese to follow.

The Party tried to whip up the whole thing, but this was a campaign that failed sooner than most. Most Chinese got fed up with it. There was nothing they could say openly, but when they were with their friends, they were cynical about it. This was probably the only time I heard Chinese intellectuals say that they didn't believe that such a character existed. I didn't believe that such a "hero" ever existed. It was an image invented by the Party to excite the feeling that its members should follow the army's example and become purer, more revolutionary. But there was absolutely no feeling for it; the Chinese participated only because they knew they had to.

I suppose these publications had some of the most uninspired Letters to the Editors in the world. The letters would be silly, gooey things that didn't say anything. "I enjoyed the lovely pictures and the wonderful article about China.

Good luck in the future." They would be signed R. Jones, New York, or T. S. Smith, Chicago. They were not fabrications; they were real. The man who handled the correspondence sat right behind me. They got hundreds of letters, but not very many from America or England. Mostly from Indonesia and places like that. The majority of the letter writers wanted the name and address of some beautiful girl who appeared in the magazine. A few might be critical of some aspect of the magazine. They wouldn't print those, of course; just record the name and address. Occasionally, they might print one that said a photograph wasn't clear, something like that. If they really wanted a wide readership, they should have printed the love letters.

When a crisis would occur in the world, the leadership often decided to stage a big demonstration to publicize Chinese feelings. Of course, they were only demonstrating Mao's feelings or the top Chinese leaders' feelings. There was always a time lag while the leaders checked out everything thoroughly. I was involved in some of these demonstrations. They were highly organized. Word goes out to every organization in and around Peking, telling them how many must come from Peking University, how many from the Press. If the leaders want 500,000 demonstrators, there will be 500,000. They have a committee for organizing the slogans, banners, streamers. Party branches are told what to do. They call small group meetings and members are told there will be a demonstration tomorrow morning to protest American action in such and such a place. They work half the night writing up their slogans on banners and posters. Everything is organized: The demonstrators are told where to get the buses, where they will get off, where they will march to, and the exact spot to stand in Tien-an-men Square. They even have permanent latrines built in the street. The organizers go around, take off the covers, put up canvas siding around them, open them to the water main and run a pipe out. They can hold a demonstration in just three or four hours—with a million people.

When the U.S. made the Russians withdraw all their missiles from Cuba, the Chinese organized great demonstrations that went on for more than a week—constantly, day and night, with millions of people. Outwardly, they were directed against the United States, but in reality they were aimed at Russia for backing down. In China, the affair was called "The Sellout of Cuba" or "The Retreat of the Russians in Cuba."

The small group of foreigners who worked with the Chinese politically were asked by the Chinese to organize all the foreigners to join the demonstrations. That's how I was brought into them. I joined the demonstrators because if you didn't join, you'd be on the blacklist and your treatment would be harsher. Most foreigners either wanted to join or had to. I was in this missile-crisis demonstration, too. I carried a placard that said: "Defend Freedom of the Seas."

We were carried down by buses, and we just walked around the corner, handed a letter to the Cubans, then walked back around the corner, got on the buses and went back to work. They made it very convenient for the foreigners. The Chinese, of course, had to walk miles.

During my years in China, I signed a couple of statements demanding that the United States stay out of Vietnam. This was mostly in 1960 and '61. I also acted a small part in a Chinese propaganda film. I played an American soldier; I was the epitome of an imperialist soldier, shooting my way through China. That was in 1961 when I was still at Peking University. I was married and we were living very frugally during the hard times. I was approached by Sid Shapiro, one of the members of the foreign group that works with the Chinese; he's a former American and has Chinese citizenship. Later I was offered 500 *yuan*, which is about 250 dollars at the official rate, a lot of money there, especially when I was on a 100-*yuan* per month stipend. We needed the money.

I had some doubts about doing the acting after all the trouble I'd had with our marriage. The main reason I did it was for the money and the hope that when I needed something during the hard times, I would get it. If you refuse them and then ask for some little thing that you need, you won't get it. Shapiro and another American, Gerald Tannenbaum, also played in the film. Tannenbaum played an American general. In one scene, I came roaring up to a checkpoint, jumped out of a truck and shot the Chinese Communist guard. From an American point of view, nothing I said was anti-American—I was shooting Communists, putting them in jail—but, of course, the theme of the film was anti-American. Even before I left China, I regretted having done it.

Mobilizing the people is one of the great tools of the Chinese Communists, as the Red Guard movement demonstrated once again after I had left China. One particularly delightful example of the value of this technique occurred during the economic hard times. There apparently was a minor clerk in Peking who had access to blank checks. He practiced signing Chou En-lai's signature until he got very good at it. Then he took a blank check, made it out for 250,000 *yuan*, signed Chou En-lai's name, got on his bicycle and pedaled down to the Central Bank. He walked in, handed over the check and said he wanted the money in cash. The bank was not about to question Chou's signature. They gave him the money, and he came out of the bank with two bags full of currency. He put it on his bicycle and rode off.

Later that afternoon, the check made its way to somebody higher up at the bank, who called Chou En-lai's office and was told no such check had been made out. The officials immediately organized all the Party branches, street committees, everybody. Everybody's house was searched—everybody's. This was done in little more than a day. They found nothing. So they ordered a more thorough search. Everybody's place was searched again; foreign students were searched in a way so that they would not know about it. This

131

time they also searched offices, and they found a slip of paper on which this man had been practicing Chou En-lai's signature. In a few days, they had him.

I suppose the most dramatic example of how the leadership could mobilize the people, what they call the "mass line," was the Ssu Ching Movement, a development of the Socialist Education Movement. It started in the winter of 1963 when Wang Kuang-mei, the wife of Liu Shao-chi, the chairman of the government, had to go to the countryside for her month of physical labor. Everyone in China has to do this. She went to a commune near Peitaiho on the sea, and she went in disguise, something like just Comrade Wong from Peking who has come to do her month's work. So she would not attract attention. She lived with a very poor peasant family; only the wife was there, the husband was missing. At first, the wife wouldn't say where her husband was. Eventually, the wife and Wang Kuang-mei became good friends and the peasant woman confided in her. She explained that they had had a daughter and the Party Secretary of the commune had liked her, gotten special favors for her and finally asked her to come and live with him. The family objected, but the Party Secretary told them it was none of their business, the daughter was over eighteen and could do what she liked.

Well, the husband decided to go over the Secretary's head and went to see the leader of the County Committee. The committee called back down to the commune and told the Party Secretary that they had received this complaint and if it was true, he would have to straighten himself out. As soon as he got word, the Party Secretary framed something against this woman's husband and had him arrested and sent away.

Wang Kuang-mei thought this was terrible, but the peasant woman told her things like that were happening all the time at this commune and other communes around there. And she told the woman, who she thought was just "Comrade Wang," about graft and people on the commune setting up private enterprises on the side and running them for a profit. Wang Kuang-mei kept quiet but when she left this place and returned to Peking, she reported to her powerful husband about it. He had her write up a report that was presented to the Central Committee of the Party. It told how the countryside was more or less falling apart with graft and corruption. The Central Committee discussed the report, sent out investigators and found that what she had said was true. There had been earlier reports of things like this but they had always been referred back down the line and things had been hushed up.

The Central Committee ordered that a condensed form of the report be read to everyone in China, all 750 million of them. All Chinese were called to meetings of small groups and organizations. My wife had to attend three long sessions. They were not allowed to take notes. No foreigners were supposed to know about it. It was to be very secret. But still my wife had to go; sometimes the right hand didn't know what the left hand was doing. The report didn't say that Liu Shao-chi's wife had started it; I learned that from my friends in high positions who knew. But that's how the Ssu Ching phase of the Socialist Education Movement started in the fall of 1964 to clean up the corruption in the countryside and later in the cities, too.

That fall they sent out thousands of people from the various organizations to ferret out corrupt officials. Two of the five people in my section went—Chinese only. My wife's brother went. They went out as "work teams" and lived with the poor peasants to gain their confidence and gather every bit of information they could. They wanted to wipe out the peasants' fear of the local Party Secretary and to administer justice. It was an experimental program at first. Each group went for at least six months and when they returned, a new group went out. The worst local leaders were sent away to camps. I'm told that the great majority of local Party Secretaries were demoted, left there and watched. The whole experience matched Mao's theory: News came from the bottom of the society to the top, and the top took action that had repercussions at the bottom.

When "work teams" came back from the countryside, I had long talks with some of them and was told how they lived, one to a family, with poor peasants and worked beside them and drew out of them all the information they could. They checked the records of the commune and in the evenings the team would get together and pool their information. They organized Poor Peasant Associations to "struggle" against Party cadres pointed out by the work teams—not the big-shots but the minor officials. The team members I talked with knew that the big-shots were getting away with it.

As more and more corruption was uncovered, the leaders recognized that it was the key Party officials who were corrupt. Mao Tse-tung and Liu Shao-chi disagreed how the problem should be handled. Liu started an intensive campaign against lower-level Party leaders, which the Chinese called "The 54 Days of White Terror." He was trying to protect the Party leadership and the organization. The mayor of Peking was one who resisted the work teams and tried to protect his officials. He had a loyal, well-knit organization. But Mao, as head of the Party, wanted to purge the people really responsible. He lost this debate in the Politburo of the Party, which voted to purge only the lower levels. But Mao declared the Party was unable to purge itself and he announced the formation of the Red Guards. He tried to use students as an outside instrument to rectify the Party and attack the key people at all levels. Liu opposed this, but in the eyes of the ordinary Chinese, Mao was trying to get rid of corrupt Party despots.

At the celebration for the fifth anniversary of the founding of the *Peking Review* magazine, in the spring of 1963, I met Chou En-lai. A lot of the top echelon leaders came out to the Foreign Languages Press for the celebration. In the big dining hall where the Chinese ate, we foreigners were scattered around at small tables with some Chinese. Chou En-lai sat down at each table in turn, spending ten to twenty minutes at each. He had been well briefed and knew that I had come from Korea, that I had been one of those who had refused repatriation, that I had been in Peking University. I talked with him mostly in Chinese but occasionally a word or two of English. He knows English. He asked me what I was doing and how I liked it. We talked about Peking University and about my wife.

The thing that really impressed me most were his shifty eyes. You couldn't hold his eyes steady; he wouldn't look you straight in the eye and hold it. It was also interesting that while he was there he drank nothing but some special tea. One of his aides kept it in a little pot and filled his glass from time to time. Chou asked me if I intended to go back to the United States and whether I had any friends who wanted to come over to China. I said I did intend to go back some day, and there were probably plenty of people who would like to come to China but couldn't. He said that was because the U.S. Government wouldn't let them come.

From my own meeting with him and from people I know who are very close to him, I believe he is intelligent and one of the leaders most well-read in foreign literature and foreign newspapers. He is, if we can use the word, more liberal than any of the others as far as foreign relations go. At the end of the celebration that day, he gave a little speech saying that the *Peking Review* had done good work in opposing American imperialism and in exposing the defeat of the revisionists—the Russians.

On our second wedding anniversary, Kai-yen and I had planned to eat out and celebrate a bit. But then President Kennedy was assassinated. I was one of the first around the Foreign Language Press to hear about it. I made it a habit at 7:30 every morning to listen to the shortwave news from Manila over a station run by a church group from America.

That morning there was a lot of static so I switched stations and finally caught the tail end of the Voice of America news. I wasn't paying too much attention. I was shaving and suddenly it dawned on me that the announcer was saying that somebody had been assassinated and it sounded like he said President Kennedy. I couldn't catch any more.

I waited and at 8 heard a news report over the Far Eastern station of the Armed Forces Radio and Television Network in Tokyo. I heard very clearly that President Kennedy had been assassinated. I had grown to like Kennedy; he represented a fresh spirit. I was dumbfounded. I had to sit down. I told Kai-yen what I had heard; she was shocked.

In the office I didn't say anything because I thought everyone had heard the news. In our office we had one Party member in charge of the section, another old man from Canton who was sort of indifferent and just did his work, and a woman we called Dora Chang, who was the daughter of a member of the Chinese Central Committee and who had graduated from a girl's college in America. Around ten o'clock someone came in and announced Kennedy's death. All three members of the section reacted differently. The girl was shocked. The old man only asked a couple questions; it didn't make any difference to him whether Kennedy was alive or dead. The Party member said, "Well, good riddance."

The general reaction was cautious, forced elation throughout the rest of the day. Because none of the Chinese had been told how to react yet, no one really knew what line to take. They seemed to feel it was probably best to be cautiously happy that Kennedy had been killed. It was a forced performance; they put on this act. But deep down inside, most Chinese intellectuals I knew, and especially those who had studied abroad, felt sad.

Then one of the official newspapers printed a cartoon showing Kennedy on the ground with the caption, "Kennedy bit the dust." But other countries let the Chinese know that they felt this was tasteless. After that, there were meetings of all Chinese organizations and everyone was told to keep quiet and not to express any opinion about Kennedy's death. Then you couldn't draw any Chinese out on the subject; they wouldn't express any feeling. But even when I left, most Chinese certainly still thought there was a political plot involved.

The foreign embassies in Peking reacted quite differently from the official attitude of the Chinese. I had many friends in the embassies, and everyone was moved. In all the embassies, the communist ones too—Russian, Polish, Yugoslav—they expressed their regrets. The Chinese never did.

America is China's chief enemy and all her efforts are directed against America. Kennedy had been the personification of her chief antagonist. On the other hand, he was clever in dealing with the Chinese and Russians; the Chinese realized this and the leaders were probably glad that he was gone.

In China, I thought Kennedy was too liberal toward communism; at the Bay of Pigs he was too liberal in not allowing the U.S. Air Force to give the troops air cover. That is exactly what the Chinese would want. The more liberal someone is toward them, the more opportunity they have to advance their cause. They'll take advantage of any opportunity given them.

The Chinese didn't think President Johnson as clever as Kennedy was. They didn't think he knew how to employ his diplomatic service as well as Kennedy could and did. But they were fearful that Johnson was more apt to use force and would be less afraid to use force than Kennedy. This tended to make them more cautious, even in Vietnam.

At this stage in history, I have come to believe, the firmer we are with China the better. Of course, we've got to let them know that we are going to be firm. We have to prove it. Then the more cautious their policy will be toward us.

X

POLICE, PLACES AND PAWNS

In the summer of 1959, I went on a vacation to Peitaiho, on the seashore not far from Peking. I didn't want to go alone so I managed to talk one of our group, who I will call Mike, into going with me. Sidney Shapiro came a few days later. Peitaiho had the reputation of being a nice resort, set aside mainly for foreigners and Chinese officials. We got our tickets and our police permits, but we didn't make any hotel reservations. We wrote to Alan Winnington's wife there to make reservations for us.

Early one morning we took the train, expecting to be there before dark, but it started raining (it had been raining off and on for a couple of weeks already), and we finally pulled into the station about midnight. The station was several miles from town and the old beat-up bus ran only during the daytime. So my friend Mike and I asked help from the railroad officials, and he put us into a sort of guest room next to the tracks. I took the sofa because it was the biggest, but even so we had to put a couple of chairs together so I could stretch out. We didn't get any sleep; just as we dozed off, along would come an engine whistling and steaming, huffing and puffing. Next morning we cleaned up as best we could and went to catch the bus. It was packed; they couldn't have gotten another person on if they wanted to. The next bus would not arrive for a couple of hours, so we managed to hire pedicabs and after a couple hours got to the hotel. We thought

Mrs. Winnington had made a reservation for us, but the hotel didn't know anything about us. Since we were foreigners and they did have empty rooms, they had to give us one.

In China all foreigners are very closely watched. They are restricted to the area in which they live, but in their area—Peking in my case—they are free to move about as much as they want. Of course, the foreigner sticks out like a sore thumb; you can't go anywhere without being recognized as different, so life is difficult. You never really can become one of the Chinese.

When a foreigner travels, he has to get a permit from the police, and it has to be stamped when you get on a train and when you get off. And you have to report to the police station within hours after you arrive at a place. In Peitaiho, we went to report; and like in all police stations in China, there were only a couple of people hanging around, and they didn't know what to do. They said a man who knew how to stamp the permit wouldn't be in for a long time. We had to wait, and when he came in, he took his own good time about stamping it. He was showing the usual arrogance of Chinese cops.

We spent the next several days swimming, and played roulette in the Winnington's villa in the evenings. I introduced my friend to a Chinese girl whom I knew from Peking. She was staying at our hotel. They started seeing quite a bit of each other and going swimming together. So I left them alone and went swimming by myself.

The hotel has its own watchers to keep an eye on all the residents and to make sure they were living a clean, moral life. These watchers reported to the police that Mike and the girl were seeing too much of each other, and one night the cops came up to the room. Mike was out and I was playing bridge with some Chinese in our room. The cops asked for everyone's credentials and asked to see my friend. He hadn't come back. So two of them waited downstairs.

Mike came in about 11:30 and we were sitting alone in the

room talking, when about midnight, up came these two cops. They just banged on the door, marched in and asked to see our papers. They already knew who we were; we were registered with them. But they take your certificate and without looking at it, ask your name and age, where you are from, where you work, what you are doing here. They want you to say all this to humble you.

When they got through with that, they told us to sit down and gave us a lecture about the laws governing aliens in China. They went on for about an hour. They wanted to frighten us, but they never mentioned the girl.

They didn't frighten my friend or the girl either. They continued to see each other. One evening a couple of nights later, they were sitting on a bench near the sea and suddenly out from the bushes jumped the same two cops and an army shore patrol guard. Guns in hand. They held a light in their eyes and asked them what they were doing there. They had to show their papers and got another lecture.

The police disapproved of the girl going out with a foreigner. The next day they sent a note to the hotel telling the girl that they wanted to see her at the police station. When a cop came for her, Mike suspected trouble so he insisted on going along. The cop tried to make him stay behind. They had a terrible row. But he followed them right to the police station, and when the police took the girl upstairs, he sat downstairs in the hall. They kept her hour after hour, and he sat there hour after hour.

He began making a nuisance of himself. He sang and annoyed a couple of people sitting in the office. He kept telling the police he wasn't leaving until the girl came down. He kept this up all day, until about 8 at night when they finally released her and the two of them came back to the hotel. He had saved her right there. They would have sent her to jail if he hadn't been there. That would have been it. Now she was frightened half out of her wits—so frightened that we packed our bags and went back to Peking with her the next day.

The police are a dreadful annoyance in China, especially to foreigners. You have to go to the police station periodically and have your foreign resident certificate stamped. Even that can be a terrible experience if they have it in for you. When I went in the early years, when my stock wasn't so bad, they just treated me with indifference.

The Peking police station is an old, cold, dark place: a small room with a couple of benches on each side and wooden tables where you can write and a very high desk behind which the police sit. The desk is so high that the average Chinese has to strain to see over the top. It was made high so you will be automatically humbled. I'm rather tall and I resented the arrangement they had, so every time I went there, I would purposely lean over the desk and peer down on them. They hated that.

The police will never make the slightest motion that will compromise their position of great authority. They are that huge unapproachable thing—the law. I remember one time I had to have the damned little red book stamped again. I walked up to the desk. A young girl was behind it. She was looking down at her work, and I just leaned over and waited and slapped my book down to see how long it would take her to look up at me and ask what I wanted. I stood there fifteen minutes—fifteen whole minutes. It got so embarrassing that her face got all red. She was not going to compromise by saying something first. It became embarrassing for all of them. Finally, one of the others broke the tension by coming over and asking me in a very rough voice, "What can we do for you? What do you want?" That saved her face.

The police are the representatives of the great Communist state of China; they are the law and every foreigner dreads facing them. You are supposed to come in there on your hands and knees, trembling, hand your red book over and have it stamped. Each time, I asked to have my book validated for five years, but when I got it back, it would only be stamped for one. They would say: We decided that if we want to give you a year, then we will give you a year and that's all.

When they inspect your credentials, they take your book and hold it without looking at it. They already know who you are but they ask you your name, age, where you are from, where you work. They know all this but they want you to say it anyway. This is to put you in your place. They act like warlords. They want to frighten you; then you are supposed to be sufficiently afraid so that you will be careful. The ordinary attitude of Chinese cops is one of arrogance—arrogance and haughtiness with foreigners.

Each year my stock with the Communists was going down and I was getting rougher treatment from the police. I got more and more fed up with the treatment, with my friends getting into trouble, innocent people being thrown into jail, girls being spirited away. Whenever I met an official, I would tell him about the treatment in the police station and how despotic they were, how fascist in their attitude. I used to refer to them as Nazis. Finally, one year I found that they had renovated the whole room at the police station, put in more lights and built another desk, much taller, so that even I could just about peek over the top.

Of course, a foreign visitor who is invited to China doesn't have to deal with the police. His interpreter or the organization that has invited him does that for him. So he never has any contact with these people. Visitors like Edgar Snow or Felix Greene, who come out writing praise for the Chinese, never get the police treatment.

Over the years, I saw much of China. We started out in Taiyüan in the west, of course, and in the earliest years I traveled to Tientsin and Dairen. During other vacations I visited cities and resorts like Tsingtao, Peitaiho and Wenchuan. At Tsingtao, which I visited with a Yugoslav friend on a summer vacation in 1957, I remember being chased by Russian and Polish girls there on vacation; they chased any foreigner, hoping to get married. They especially wanted to marry me because I was an American and they wanted to get to America. I was a bit fearful of them really; they were so aggressive. One night a girl even broke into my hotel room. When we first arrived, a painter was doing some work in my room and this well-built Chinese girl slithered into my room, very catlike. My Chinese was still poor then, but I understood her asking the painter who I was. He told her I was a foreign student from Peking and that I was an American. I didn't speak to her, so she couldn't speak to me; that's Chinese etiquette. She left. That evening after I wrote a letter, I went to bed and shoved a huge heavy chair against the door because I had a large sum of money on me and I couldn't lock the door. During the night there was a fierce storm, thunder and lightning, and I woke up and heard someone trying to force open my door. I thought they were trying to rob me, so I jumped up and held the chair against the door. Whoever it was finally gave up, and through the window I could see her going away—it was that same Chinese girl.

In 1963 the Red Cross took those of us who still remained in China on a month-and-a-half trip up and down the central part of China. By now the Chinese had decided that any foreigners who wanted to leave China would be allowed to go, and they decided to give everybody a marvelous, free trip around the country—red-carpet treatment. Anything you wanted for a month and a half, and as soon as that was over, anyone who wanted to go, go.

Once this decision had been made, their whole treatment of us changed. They became friendly and tried to sugarcoat us, especially the three who were leaving China. On this trip there were a couple of other nationals and eight Americans: Howard Adams, Clarence Adams, Belhomme, Skinner, Rush, White, Veneris [ex-Pfc. James G. Veneris of Vandergrift, Pennsylvania] and myself. All the rest had gone home already. We traveled to Canton and then all through central China and stayed in the best places. We took long trips on a number of rivers.

After a while the group was split up, and White, Veneris and I went by car across the province of Kiangsi and visited a small town where porcelain had been made for hundreds of years. We met up with the other group at a mountain resort named Lushan, Chiang Kai-shek's private summer resort, a very beautiful place where we stayed nearly a week. Then we continued up the Yangtze by riverboat to Wuhan and then on to Chengchow and to Loyang where the Buddhist grottoes are.

On the way, we visited the old home of Mao Tse-tung, where he was born. The Chinese have downgraded his birth as much as possible. They've tried to cover up. But if anyone goes and looks at his former home, as I did, he would know that his family was a big landlord family. Of course, in the official papers they say his family was just a rich peasant family, but that's wrong. They were a landlord family; there's no question about it.

More than 85 percent of those in power in China are from aristocratic families, mainly landlord families, and a small percentage, like Chou En-lai, from upper-middle-class families from the cities. The aristocracy was the only class that had the money and could afford to give their children an education. Real, honest-to-goodness working people the Chinese never had; all they had besides the aristocrats were the peasants.

We also visited Taiyüan, the place we'd first gone to nearly ten years earlier. It had changed so much I didn't even recognize it. Wide avenues, paved now; modern brick buildings had gone up all over. The little mud houses were torn down. The city was very clean now, well planned with a lot of factories. Anything we wanted to visit, we could visit. We spoke Chinese and could talk with anyone we wanted to. Nothing was prohibited except the military things you wouldn't even ask for.

The trip did mellow us a bit. We weren't so anticommunist or anti-Chinese when we returned. Conditions had been so hard in the previous two or three years that we had gotten a distorted view of what the rest of China was like. We came back with the impression that the country was not so bad off and the people were not as antiregime as we had thought. We found the people in the countryside more satisfied than we had expected. The three among us who had wanted to leave—Rush, Skinner and Belhomme—did leave, but two others, Clarence Adams and Howard Adams, who were wavering, decided to stay after this trip. White, Veneris and I were not ready to leave. White finally left just before I did, and only three remained after I left.

The final dramatic event of the period when I worked at the Foreign Languages Press came one morning in October 1964. I was asked to check the final copy of the announcement of a nuclear explosion by the Chinese in Sinkiang Province in western China. I pointed out a number of odd phrases and commented that it could not have been a bomb as the copy said; it must have been only a "nuclear device." The editors called somewhere and confirmed that it had to be a bomb. The fact that the Chinese wanted to stress so strongly that it was a bomb made me think—knowing the Chinese character—that they wouldn't have insisted so much if it really had been a bomb.

When this first "bomb" was exploded, the Chinese I knew were just brimming with elation. I was always against the proliferation of nuclear weapons and nuclear nations; but they would say: We're Chinese and we have been able to make a bomb and we are just as good as the white man. There is throughout China, especially among officials and intellectuals, still a feeling of inferiority.

There is absolutely no question that the Chinese had given top priority to their nuclear-weapons program, even during the hard times, even if it meant starving a million or two million people. Their nuclear industry had been going at top speed right along. There is no question in my mind that China will develop more bombs than the United States or Russia in a shorter time because so much of her energy is concentrated on that goal—to give China equality with the white man.

But I doubt that the Chinese will threaten to use their bombs. That is what they have accused the Russians of doing. They will just let us know that they have them and can use them. I believe that ever since 1958, when it became clear to the Chinese that the Russians were not going to give them nuclear bombs or even enough technical assistance to make one, Chinese policy has been to cause a war between the United States and Russia.

Late in 1964, my Chinese friend who worked in Chou En-lai's office told me that the reason Mao disappeared from the news so often was that he had built in remote southwest China, outside the city of Yaan, a huge secret war head-quarters. It was cut into the earth—seven stories deep—with computers and all sorts of elaborate equipment. Mao spent much of his time there. It was near a lake where Mao had a villa and could go boating. I was told that Mao sat at a desk on a platform that acted like an elevator and could carry him to any level. In recent years, many secret meetings were held there. Outside, the headquarters was all painted white, supposedly to reflect radiation. White buildings are rare in China; usually buildings are left their natural color.

I found that the Chinese scientists who are working on the bomb are not allowed in Peking. They have their own place, a special town built for them, out in the provinces—well supplied. They have chauffeur-driven cars and are well paid and well taken care of. Of course, they are watched and restricted. My understanding is that they are all Chinese, except that I heard rumors about an American woman who was supposed to be helping the Chinese. I have met her parents, who were missionaries, and her brother. The story I heard was that in her early days she worked in New Mexico and had some connection with the development of the first American atomic bomb. Her parents came to China in 1958 to visit her and her children. I remember them saying that their daughter was supposed to be in Inner Mongolia, working on a farm there helping to develop some sort of agriculture, but that in reality she was in the western part of China working with the Chinese on a scientific project. Later I heard several times from the elite group of procommunist foreigners that she was connected with China's nuclear project.

Over the years, I became familiar with this elite group of English-speaking foreigners, including maybe fifteen Americans, who have thrown in their whole lives with the Chinese. Many of them have been in China for many years, some even as far back as 1940 and earlier. Other languages have their own similar groups. They have been in China long enough so that they've learned to play the game. They do or say only what they think the Party will like; I'd say that 90 percent of them are only in for what they can get out of it. Their aim is to climb as high as they can over the top of others. That's why it doesn't bother them when the Chinese change their policy from black to white overnight. Their only motive is to keep themselves politically in tune with the Chinese leaders, regardless. They work with the Chinese hand-in-glove, and the Chinese use them. They became very much involved in Vietnam and in stirring up any trouble they could in England and America.

They are the end result of Communist indoctrination over a long period of time. The longer you go through this indoctrination, the more clever you become. It contradicts the whole purpose of criticism-and-self-criticism. These people are very perceptive; if they see a chance to knock off a superior, or step into his shoes, they'll do it. Most of these "elite" foreigners are like that. They have completely cut themselves off from the West. Most of them have taken Chinese citizenship and have joined the Chinese Communist Party. Now they have no place else to go.

The members of this group are used as sort of a front. They attend conferences; they have been sent abroad many times. They help with foreign visitors, drafting documents, getting experts into China and influencing their views. Whenever they get together, they sing those old Spanish Civil War songs.

The leader of this group is Michael Shapiro, an Englishman on the lam. He has a direct liaison with the Central Committee of the Chinese Communist Party. Among the Americans are Sydney Rittenberg, a former Methodist from Charleston, South Carolina, and Dr. George Hatem, who has been working with the Communists since the late 1930's. Of course, the top American is Anna Louise Strong, but she's grown old, and Julian Schuman puts out a newsletter under her name. Sidney Shapiro is an American who was discharged from the U.S. Army while he was in China and had a love affair with a woman who was an underground Party agent. He plays the game so well that he has made many enemies. Two others among the Americans are Joan Hinton and Gerry Tannenbaum in Shanghai. About 1958 an American Treasury Department official named Frank Coe defected to China and was kept under cover. I met Coe, and when I came out of China he was one of the people our government asked me about. Another member of this group is Israel Epstein, who was refused American citizenship during World War II and is very bitter about that. He was born in China and has Chinese citizenship and is very anti-American.

Epstein is one of the Chinese links to America for organizing campus sit-ins and demonstrations. Late one night in May 1965, I overheard Epstein making a telephone call. My kitchen window faced his bedroom. The windows were open and he was talking loudly, telling his small-group leader his impressions of two American ladies who had just been in North Vietnam. He had just come from a Peking-duck dinner with Anna Louise Strong and Rewi Alley, a New Zealander who has lived in China for a very long time. Epstein explained that someone in England had contacted these women in New York, and they had slipped in through Russia and now they were going back to help the Chinese set up contacts in New

York and in Washington to get more support for China. Usually, this is easier to do from England, less expensive, and it's legal that way.

Another man who worked on relations with English-speaking peoples was an Englishman who had gone to a university in the United States and fought in the Spanish Civil War. He had fought for the British in World War II and stayed in China, making his way to Yenan where he knew Mao. He was well-educated and well-read and later taught at the Foreign Languages Institute in Peking. In 1966 he was lecturing in England and Canada, and I was surprised to find that he even visited the United States.

The Chinese tried to inspire a lot of campus objections in the United States to the Vietnam war. They were doing everything they could. They didn't bridge the Pacific; they worked mostly through England and had contacts there and in America, too. This was talked about in Peking all the time.

There was always a dribble of Americans coming to and going from Peking—not just ordinary tourists. They sneak into Peking all the time, and very often go on down to North Vietnam. In Peking this is known as "the milk run." The Americans who sneak into Communist China are often people who have some contact with this elite group. They go to Russia or come to the Chinese border, and the Chinese issue them a special piece of paper to tack onto their passport. I remember an architect some time ago, and there were the two ladies from New York; they had just ordinary jobs but may have been undercover of some kind. Certainly they got propaganda into the United States.

While I was in school, I had little contact with this elite group because as a foreign student they had nothing to do with me. Once I got to the Press, I found that these people more or less controlled everything connected with foreigners there. As soon as I arrived, Sid Shapiro came to visit me and he indicated politely that it would be advisable if I joined their study group. He explained that the English-speaking foreigners at the Foreign Languages Press and in Peking had two study groups, one of English and one of Americans. So I joined the American group. We met once a week during office hours and went out to a restaurant and discussed current problems. Sometimes they would order in all sorts of food and drink and sit in one of our apartments and talk. They made a nice day of it. Of course, you always had to criticize America and praise China. I kept quiet.

Early in 1963 we studied articles by Mao. In one, he blasted the Russians and said that nuclear war wasn't anything to be feared, that it would not wipe out mankind; if 300 million Chinese were killed, they would still have 300 million left. After this had been read to our group, each person was asked to give a little talk. I was given the question, "Would a nuclear war wipe out mankind?" I waited till the next week to answer and when it came my turn, I blasted Mao's theory. I said the great possibility was that the whole world's population would be wiped out, not from the blast but from the fallout. There would be hideous mutations and mankind might be wiped out completely. I went on like that for about half an hour. Their faces got redder and redder. They couldn't answer me. When I was through, they said I should study more of Mao's works and they called the meeting to a close.

Soon afterward, Sid Shapiro came around handing out tickets to the swimming pool at the Friendship Hotel. I wasn't included. The next week when there was a meeting, I didn't go. Sid came around, and I told him I was through with the study group and probably with China.

From that time, I was really an outcast. They didn't trust me at all. At times they would still try to draw me back into their meetings. I wasn't absolutely hopeless from their point of view. But they didn't know what to do with me. That is a basic difference between Russian and Chinese Communism: the Chinese principle that everyone can be saved ideologically. This is the idea behind the self-criticism meetings and the jailings without fixed sentences. If they can transform your ideology, you won't commit that crime against society again. You will be saved.

Right after the Americans began bombing North Vietnam in 1965, Michael Shapiro and a few others of the elite group called a meeting of all English-speaking resident foreigners in Peking. Or all those from whom they thought they could get support. I thought I would go, out of curiosity, and see what was going on. I found their meeting room packed and most of the elite group present. Michael Shapiro called the meeting to order and said that the Central Committee of the Party wanted the foreigners in Peking to show more enthusiasm for Chinese support of the North Vietnamese in the war. He explained that they had called this meeting to discuss what more they could do to develop the movement in America— on the campuses, among Negroes, and anything else they could think of.

There were suggestions about making recordings to send to North Vietnam and South Vietnam. In South Vietnam they would be broadcast to the American soldiers. Others suggested writing letters and propaganda sheets and getting those into America by various means. A select committee was appointed to provide the means. They wanted to bring as many professors and students as possible into the chain. The Chinese envisioned that the start would be made on the campuses; the Party saw the war coming to a halt because of this movement in America.

Over the years, I grew to dislike a large number of the members of this elite group—not all of them, I must say. But many of them make life so miserable for a foreigner in China, spying and reporting on him. They would report on me, report who my friends were, who I had seen and Lord knows what stories they made up. They are eager pawns of the Communists.

XI

THE RETURN

Even before my attack on Mao's theory, I had had enough experiences to realize that I could not stay in China. I was terribly disillusioned with China and its methods; the objectives that communism has for a person's life, or the life of the family, still look good—on paper.

The worst experience, of course, was Kai-yen's arrest. Another major crisis occurred in the winter of 1963 when I became ill. I was working at the Press at the time. Our apartment was very cold, and we sat around with all our clothes on, shivering. We only got heat once in the morning and once in the evening at that time. I caught cold and one evening passed blood from my kidneys. This frightened me.

The next morning I went to our dispensary to see about visiting a hospital. They made me fill out a slip and told me how to go to the hospital. They informed me that I would get the same treatment that all Chinese do. I said if that's all I get, that's all I get. I didn't know what was coming.

The hospital was in a slum. It was very dirty outside. Inside were hundreds of people milling around in a little crowded hallway—all sorts of people—old, crippled, filthy, ragged with sores. A disgusting sight. I finally managed to get myself registered and was told to stand on a line behind at least fifty people. There were only two doctors and they were working continuously.

Inside was just as cold as it was outside. Windows out,

filth all over the floors, piles of paper, the bathroom indescribable. A disgusting, stinking place. And this was typical of the hospitals for the ordinary Chinese. Medical care for the high Party leaders and for the invited foreign experts is as good in China as it is here. But for the ordinary Chinese, it is very, very crude. The medical treatment I was getting was on the level of what the ordinary Chinese had.

I waited there four hours before I got to the doctor. He just sent me upstairs for a urine test. Finally, he decided he didn't know what was wrong with me and wanted to pass me on to someone else. But I wasn't going through that again.

I went straight to the Red Cross and told them I wasn't going back there. They wrote out permission for me to go to another hospital, where the big Chinese officials and the foreign experts go. This is the hospital that Felix Greene and Edgar Snow write about in their books. I went there the next day and was told I would be able to register only as an ordinary patient and could not use the experts' special section or the special section for high Chinese officials. I managed to see a doctor; he didn't know what was wrong either and made an appointment for me to come back. I never went back.

This experience really shook me. I realized I could get something seriously wrong with me, I could die, and they wouldn't give a damn. I made up my mind that I had to leave soon. I began to think concretely about how to get out. This was the decisive thing. I wasn't very "progressive" by this time, but at least I was still trying to be neutral. Now this threw me even to the right of neutral. I was on my way to the feeling I have today.

Fortunately, when our baby girl, Linda, was born in July 1964, Kai-yen was registered at the Peking Maternity Hospital. It is a clean hospital, probably one of the cleanest in Peking. We were lucky. We had gone there and registered six months before the baby was due; once a mother is registered, that's where the baby will be born. Kai-yen had checkups every week; the same doctor each time, a woman doctor, and she did the delivery too. It is a strict hospital. Husbands are only allowed in on Sundays. I went downstairs while Kai-yen was delivering, and they wouldn't let me go up afterward. That was the rule.

During this entire period, my situation in China was getting more difficult. The position of the Chinese in relation to all foreigners, and to Americans in particular, was becoming clearer. At one time, while I was a prisoner in Korea, I had been useful to them. Once I had gone into China, the fact that I had refused repatriation didn't mean anything to them; that became more and more evident. As time went on, it became increasingly apparent that they didn't want me, that I was no longer useful to them, and the clearer this became to me, the more dissatisfied I became with the Chinese. By 1963 or so I felt useless. By the end, they just tolerated me.

I suppose I am the lone-wolf type. I always tried to stay pretty much to myself; I tended to be cautious, conservative. In China everything worked to draw you into the collective society and I was an independent type of person. That comes, I think, from my background as the Chinese have accused me—being of "peasant" origin.

One incident that showed this clash between the Communist drive toward collectivism and my independent instincts occurred while Kai-yen was pregnant and we were at the Foreign Languages Press. Because she didn't belong to any organization or any small group, she came automatically under the control of the Street Committee. One morning I didn't feel well and hadn't gone to work. I was in the kitchen when a woman, the head of the Street Committee, opened our door and stuck her head in and shouted that there was a meeting over in the big dining hall. So I stuck my head around the corner of the kitchen door and shouted back at her, almost in her ear, that no one was going to any damned meeting, and to get out. She was surprised and apologized to me and said she didn't know I was there. Then

154

she said very politely: They are having a meeting and your wife should go. I said: She's pregnant and don't come here asking her to go to any more meetings. That's final! She shut the door and left. The Street Committee doesn't want to get involved with foreigners; they don't know what they are getting into. They never came back.

In China you can always tell exactly where a person stands by the way he's addressed. There is a central organization that classifies all foreigners. The highest form of address is "Lao," meaning elder or respected. Then comes "Comrade." Next below, in my case while I was in the university, was "Fellow Student," and below that just "Friend." I went through all but the highest stage. In the beginning, I was Comrade and by 1957 at Peking University I went down to Fellow Student. By the end of 1958, I was just Friend. Then they dropped me all the way down to "Mister," the lowest category. I complained to the Red Cross and they put me back up to Friend. At the Press, I was officially an office worker, *Kung-tso Jen-yuan.* Then in 1964, until I left, I became Mister again.

All these things together made me realize that I would have to be going. The Chinese had indicated, I felt, that they didn't care anymore whether I stayed or not. I was a burden. When I first went to the Press, I got along all right with the other people in my section who were all Chinese. I was still a bit progressive and tried to see their view. But as time went on, I became quieter and quieter, more and more resolved to get out. They felt this, of course, so our relations became cool.

In June 1964, my two-year contract at the Press would run out, as I understood it. I asked the editorial board about renewing it, and they told me I had another six months to go, because the first six months had been on a trial basis. In the next months, I asked repeatedly about the contract—asked for a raise and for better medical care. I got no word. They knew I was very dissatisfied with the Press and the Chinese in general. Of course, I could have stayed forever on the old

155

basis, but they were obviously not prepared to give me the raise I thought I deserved. In January 1965, I asked the Red Cross about the contract, and when I never heard from them on it, I decided to go.

I contacted the American Consulate in Hong Kong through the British in Peking and went through all the procedures and swore an oath in front of the British. I started writing to the States and Western Europe, looking for a job where I could use my knowledge of the Chinese language.

In February 1965, I telephoned for an appointment with the Red Cross and that afternoon took a bus into town and went to their compound. I saw Yi Cheng-hsin, the man who went to Brazil to bring back the nine Chinese who were in jail there for espionage. He was my contact at the Red Cross; I used to see him about once a month. He's a typical, dogmatic bureaucratic official. When he tried to be tough, he always spoke Chinese, but I would never speak Chinese with him if I could help it. When he speaks English, he is at a disadvantage.

We sat down, and they brought us tea and cigarettes. I told him I was planning on leaving at the end of the year and that I was giving them plenty of time to make preparations. I said, "I'm telling you now so that when the time comes for me to go, I don't want you to say that you haven't had enough time." He didn't seem too surprised. He said, "Well, all right, you've lived here a long time, been in China a long time, and, of course, we would not restrict you from going. If you want to go, it's up to you; you can go, but we hope you'll reconsider."

The Chinese have an agreement signed with the Americans in Warsaw by which they have to let you go. So the possibility of their putting me in jail or causing my wife any more trouble was remote by now. Chinese policy had changed. Now they desired to get rid of foreign residents who were not wholehearted supporters of Chinese policy. Those who won't fit in, won't conform, they want to leave. I had not been conforming ideologically. My leaving would be mutually satisfactory.

Then, shortly after that, the Chinese asked me if I would teach. They knew I was interested in teaching and they were setting up a Foreign Languages Press Training School in an old orphanage way out in the Western Hills outside Peking. I was invited to teach English there. The students were all officers and men of the Chinese Army, learning various languages: French, Italian, Arabic, German, Spanish, Swahili.

The school was strange in a way. They never gave us teachers any clear answers about why the school had been set up. Living in China you learn that it's not appropriate to ask certain questions, so you don't ask. The public story was that the students had been demobilized and were going to be assimilated into different organizations, mainly the Foreign Languages Press. But the Press didn't need these people. In time, I suspected that they were going to be sent to Africa and other undeveloped areas and that some of them might be sent to North Vietnam. The school wanted only Americans as teachers of English; they wanted pure American English taught.

I agreed to go. Teaching is better work than translating. They paid me the same 234 *yuan* a month I had been making at the Press for only three or four hours work a day, instead of the eight I had worked at the Press. Whether this was an attempt to reconcile me, I don't know. They provided a big, black 1941 Buick for myself and two former Americans: Betty Chan, formerly Betty Chandler, and Sidney Shapiro. We called it "the hearse."

We would drive each day past the homes of the high Chinese leaders in Jade Springs Park, a walled area heavily guarded with mounted troops, probably one of the best-guarded places in the world. Frequently, we would pass one of the officials tearing down the road in a huge Mercedes, its windows screened with silk. There was also an airfield, with two Viscounts waiting there for any emergency. If the planes were sitting there, we would know that the officials were in Peking.

One day, coming back from the school we had a new driver for our car; this was his first day. We were just about a mile beyond Jade Springs when ahead of us we saw this night-soil cart drawn by a mule. The road was just two cars wide. Suddenly, coming toward us was this big Mercedes and right behind it a car loaded with Chinese plainclothesmen. But our driver pulled out to pass the cart. The driver of the Mercedes, seeing that our driver was going to attempt to go by, flashed the red light on the front of his car. Our driver didn't pay any attention. He started to pass the cart. The big Mercedes wouldn't stop; it came right on, went off onto the shoulder and flashed by and kept going. The car with the plainclothesmen came to a screeching halt. I thought they were ready to shoot. But because the first car kept going, they had to start up again and keep going.

At the school, I taught basic English; in fact, I was writing the textbook as I went along. I taught there until a month before I left. On September first, I gave the school notice that I would be leaving on October 10.

On September 16, I sent Kai-yen down to the police detention center in the western suburbs to ask for an exit visa. Usually, if any Chinese would walk in and ask for an exit permit, they would bully him. But Kai-yen told me later that she felt they already knew she would be coming. The word had come down to treat her well. They gave her papers to fill out, and she had to have photographs taken; she came back and filled out the papers and took them down less than a week later. I knew that if they wanted to create trouble for us, they could have refused to let her out. Then I wouldn't have gone either. I wouldn't be here.

The next day I went down to the police department that handles aliens, where I had to go every year to have my residence permit renewed. I walked in very boldly. To get my permit renewed irked me every year, because it's hell facing these people. They are mean. This time my residence permit was going to run out on September 30, so my red book had to be stamped again. I filled out the long form in Chinese and at the bottom wrote that I wanted this extended for one month. I handed it in and she said, "You mean one year here, don't you?" I said casually, "No, no. Only one month. I'm only staying one month, and while I'm here I might as well ask for an exit permit, please."

Her whole attitude changed. Now she was so sweet and nice. "Oh, Mr. Wills, can we help you? What can we do for you?" But when I went back on September 25 to pick up the permit, it wasn't ready. They kept me sitting there for half an hour; they did it purposely, another of the little incidents that plague people who aren't in favor. I got angry with her, and she said, "Don't come back here anymore. When it's ready, we'll call you." I said, "Don't wait till the last day either. I want it at least a week before I go, because I still have to go to the British." So about a week before we left, I got word to pick up my exit permit.

About two months before we expected to leave Peking, I had decided that, although I had traveled over much of China, I should get as much additional recent information as I could. I told the Red Cross that when I left, I intended to do some writing. I did it knowing full well that they would consider this in their treatment of us. I asked for visits around Peking. So they arranged for me to visit, over a period of a week, a machine-tool factory, a bakery, a commune, a rug mill and a jail.

The factory made milling machinery. A Red Cross official and I visited all of its five workshops. The deputy director who showed me around seemed to feel a bit strange speaking to a foreigner in Chinese. We visited over Chinese tea and cigarettes before touring the plant. Pinned on the workshop walls were propaganda posters with slogans: "Down with American Imperialism. Support the Vietnamese." In the foundry the men were less skilled, dirty and raggedy. There were women working there, too. One was taking red-hot chunks of steel from the furnace and carrying them to a steel hammer which pounded them into huge bolts.

The deputy director admitted there was a system of incentives, monthly bonuses—extra food, extra clothing allowances. But he tried to play it down. Everyone in China has security as far as a job goes. Once you have a job, you are secure. The only way you can be thrown out is if you commit some political mistake or a crime. Then you are sent to jail, and in any case you are looked after there too. But if you simply do a poor job, they will apply psychological pressure, hold an accusation meeting against you; and if that doesn't change you, you will be transferred to another job that is less demanding.

The next day they took me to a bakery in the old Moslem section of Peking near the jail. The same Red Cross man and I toured the plant in white smocks and white caps. It was a low-ceilinged mud building, sort of dirty, rather slummy and cramped, and the machines were very old. The workers were mainly women. They looked haggard and pallid, but they wrapped candy very fast. We learned they were on piece work. We also visited the nursery where the workers' young children are left for the day.

The following Monday we drove out to a commune made up of a number of villages. The Chinese had tried setting up classical communes in 1958—everybody getting what he needs—but this had completely fallen through. The peasants did nothing and ate everything they produced. They went back to a system where you get paid in accordance with the number of work points you accumulate. The attempt to pay workers by their needs had failed, and now the more work you did, the more you got.

Right after the Communists took over in 1949, they had sent Party members to the countryside to organize the peasants into mutual aid teams. Everyone was given some land.

The landlords either were killed or committed suicide or worked as ordinary peasants. On the commune I visited, I saw the house of a man who had formerly been a landlord. But in the beginning, the Party members organized the peasants to get them to work as a team: All of us will help you and then the next man and so on around. They would loan each other tools and draft animals, if they had one. Then the Party organized these mutual aid teams into cooperative communes with some animals and tools owned by everyone in common. Money they made would be used to buy more collective property to be used by all. Later, they collectivized the land and all the tools—everything. Then they tried to go to the final stage, where everything is owned by the collective and you do what work you can and in return get whatever you need or want; that failed. By the time of my visit, the land was still owned collectively but the peasants were being paid according to what they earned.

At this commune we visited, the people complained about a lack of rain over so many years. Water was their worst problem. Every square inch of land was cultivated; they couldn't afford to let land lie fallow. And they didn't have enough fertilizer. The place looked parched. The cotton was only a foot high when it should have been much more advanced and the winter wheat looked very, very poor.

I know from my boyhood that in the States when you have your own farm and if you work it well, you have the satisfaction of accomplishing something. But in China, you get the impression that there are masses of people struggling with the earth every minute of the day, just to get a little bit from it. But the earth is exhausted. It can't produce any more. You can't get any more out of it.

There are just too many people in China. They can't grow enough food for all those people. Every square usable inch of land is cultivated. It is one fantastic struggle with nature, just to get enough food to exist on. There's not enough land; the land doesn't get a chance to recover, so it grows less and less. The people become more desperate and work it harder and harder. Agriculture is going to be China's biggest problem for many decades.

In the past half-dozen years, the Chinese have tried to expand the cultivated areas. They have been leveling complete hills. Masses of laborers go up onto a hill and level it. That is what they were doing at this commune, leveling land. And at the same time the Chinese have tried to control the population explosion. Contraceptives were available to anyone who wanted them, sterilization was encouraged and abortion was very cheap and encouraged too. But the people in the countryside didn't give a damn about such things because it is traditional for Chinese to want a big family.

Next, I saw the number one Peking rug mill. Until 1960 the Russians had bought its production. The mill had old wooden looms and rows of workers, very shabby, many of them women. There were about ten people making one big rug, sitting there day after day, pulling threads through and across. And there were row after row after row of these groups.

The last place I visited was the Peking jail. At the gate two Chinese soldiers were standing very stiffly with their burp guns. Inside there were no bars anywhere. Corridors radiated out from a central hub where a guard could be stationed. Everything was swept clean—very military. The prisoners were all young and most were political criminals. The guards didn't have to worry about them. Once they have undergone their ideological accusations and transformation, they are completely broken, completely subdued. And once they show that they sincerely regret what they have done and that they do want to start a new life, that's the time and the only time that they would be freed.

The warden tried to give the impression that he was very open, had nothing to hide. But I could see that he was very tough, strict, ruthless in his job. We walked through the workshops where the prisoners were making sandals and stock-ings. As soon as the prisoners saw the warden coming, they would look up from their work benches with fear in their eyes, then immediately, right down with their heads and concentrate on what they were doing. They wouldn't look up again until he had gone by and then they would sort of glare at him. They showed fear and hate: fear because they knew what he could do and what he would do; hate for what he had done.

On October 10, I stopped working. We prepared to leave China. Through the wise counsel of Professor John M. H. Lindbeck, I hoped to work at Harvard University. The last weeks were busy. The school gave me a banquet. The Red Cross gave me one, in a private room at a very nice restaurant. *China Pictorial* also gave me a banquet. And all my friends did. We were on the go continually.

Our last nights in Peking were very emotional. Two evenings before we left, Kai-yen invited her relatives and all of our very closest Chinese friends to our apartment. There were about fifteen people, some of whom I had known very well for a long time. Everyone sat around listening to old songs like "Goodnight, Irene," songs like that, Western, mournful music. And they said how sad it would be when we were gone. Every fifteen minutes or so, some would break out crying. Tears. Kai-yen was going away and they would probably never see her again. Everyone was down in the dumps, feeling very low. There were long lapses with hardly a word spoken; just sitting, thinking. And the last night was like that, too, with a smaller group, her sister, her half brother and a few others. My wife cried, and I was controlling myself only with great effort. The hardest moment was each time someone left—someone who was dear to us and whom we might never see again. I would take them out and see them off. There's a phrase in Chinese—"*Yi-lu-ping-an*"—it means "peaceful journey."

We left Peking by plane on the seventeenth. The Chinese paid our fares and for our overweight baggage, too. Our friends all came to the airport, and that was one time when the Chinese and Russians came together. My good friend, the second secretary of the Russian embassy, was there with his wife. We left early in the morning, about 8. The Red Cross and the Press brought us out to the airport in a car. Our baggage had gone out the previous day. We boarded a Viscount and had a four-hour flight to Canton. Fortunately, the baby slept most of the way.

Canton was packed with foreigners. The Red Cross put us up in a good, clean hotel and wined and dined us. Two Red Cross officials showed us all around, and we visited a luxurious modern resort in the White Cloud Mountains near there. We spent most of our day and a half in Canton sightseeing. And my wife visited her brother who is a gym teacher there, training athletes. He's a good gymnast. The day we arrived Kai-yen and her brother, in the hotel lobby, accidentally bumped into their father who had come there for the annual Canton Trade Fair and was just preparing to leave for Peking. They only had time to take a walk in the park together and to talk for a while. I just looked around the city and sent off a couple of telegrams to an old friend to say goodbye and to a friend in Hong Kong to tell him I was coming.

By this time I was getting anxious. Fifteen years! I didn't know what was waiting for us. After fifteen years, it was really just like plunging. What was the other side like? Would we have our luggage stolen? How would we get down from the border to a hotel? Would there be anyone at the border?

I even thought for a moment of stopping the whole machine right there, but that would be a terrible job because I'd already gone so far. It was like a snowball from the very beginning to the end, and at the very end it was an avalanche. I had no idea what was waiting on the other side. It was like jumping off a ledge or plunging into a pool of black water.

Once things started rolling the next day, that kept me occupied. I woke up early; I hadn't slept much. Kai-yen's brother came to say goodbye. They wouldn't see each other soon again. We got on the train and the final journey started at 7:30 in the morning. It was a glorious day. The Red Cross representative slept most of the way. We arrived at the border at 10:30. I had our Chinese exit permits and our British entrance visas to Hong Kong. When the train arrived, I sat there, just sort of petrified, looking out the window. I mean, this was it! There was certainly no turning back now.

Kai-yen carried the baby and I carried the bags. The Chinese took us upstairs in a rather nice building right at the border and gave us a farewell meal. I tried to eat, but I couldn't. The others ate. Customs inspected our baggage, but the only thing they kept was a detailed map of Peking. I could not resist telling them that I already had a map like this one waiting for me in Hong Kong. I had sent it out through a neutral embassy.

Then the Chinese officials took us up to the covered bridge over the little river that separates China from Hong Kong. The border is in the middle of the bridge. We shook hands, and someone told me that anytime I wanted to come back to China, I was welcome. They let us go from there.

Kai-yen and I walked up to the border and a British immigration official [Senior Inspector Thomas A. H. Hodson] came up and asked me, "Are you Mr. Wills?" I said, "I am." And he said I had permission to enter Hong Kong for fourteen days. A British Red Cross woman [Miss Nancy Gibson] was there also, and together they took us down.

At the far end of the bridge was a U.S. consul [Nicholas Platt] and he said, "I'm glad to see you here."

He took me into a waiting room in the British building and wanted to verify that I was still an American citizen. He asked me eight questions such as: Had I taken part in any elections, had I joined any Chinese military service, had I joined any Chinese political parties?

The answers were all no.

XII

OVER MY SHOULDER

Today, when I look back over the fourteen years that followed my capture by the Chinese Communists in Korea, I am ashamed of going to China, of turning my back on the United States and on my family. But I'm not ashamed of my years in China. Once I was there, I was an American and I always felt like an American. As much as I could, without getting into trouble, I always defended the United States as well as possible. At times, if I was called upon to sign a peace appeal or something like that, I certainly could not very well have refused that.

All the Chinese I met asked me about America, and I always did what I could, bit by bit, to give them a more correct view of my country, a more realistic view. I felt guilty every time they accused the Americans of doing something. I felt that on many points the United States was being accused falsely. Which she is. But often there is no way you can defend her there without being scorned, and you know that at the same time you are being scorned back home for going there. But, of course, you are always an American.

If I had started from what I know now, I wouldn't even have volunteered for the Army. Of course, if I were drafted, I would serve; but if I ended up in a POW camp, I would not do the same thing again. I would go home. When I defected, I was angry with America for deserting us in Korea. I suffered in Korea, but I suffered in China, too, in a different way. In Korea I suffered physically; in China I suffered mentally. It's such a completely different society. You are alone, isolated—lonely. Leaving aside my wife and child, I would not have gone there if I had it to do over, if I had known then what was before me.

And yet, if not for my wife and child, I would still be there. If I hadn't wanted to get married, I wouldn't have gotten into all that trouble with the Chinese. And later a lot of irritations resulted from my being married. If I had remained single, the Chinese would have been more cautious in their treatment of me because they would have realized that I could have left anytime. But they knew they could stop my wife; that's why our treatment wasn't so easy at times. I left because the Chinese didn't treat me well enough, but I always regarded the things that displeased me as faults of the communist system.

When I first wanted to get married, I looked at it in some part as a way of becoming more integrated, of getting settled in China for a much longer stay. But after Kai-yen had been taken away and was then allowed to come back, when we got married after all that, then I knew it was only a matter of a few years before I would return.

Overseas Chinese, like Kai-yen, don't like the communist aspect of China, but it doesn't matter to them so much as China does. They take pride in China. It's a symbol of the Yellow Man being able to stand up by himself. They won't shout it but they are proud that there is a China that can stand up to the United States and Russia and *is* standing up to them—even if the principles involved don't suit them.

Kai-yen, like all the young Chinese, accepted what she was told. Most Chinese children under sixteen, I'd say, haven't really learned what the whole thing is about. But they are indoctrinated to socialism. They admire model workers or the ideal soldier like Lei Feng as our children do cowboys. Later, this would make them ripe for the Red Guard—prepared to give instantaneous and unquestioning support to Mao Tse-tung. But they don't get the self-criticism training very thoroughly during their younger years. That comes later, after they have left high school and gone either to a university or some place to work. Only then does it become vicious and ruthless.

Because Kai-yen automatically accepted what she was told, if the *People's Daily* said the United States had bombed a certain place or killed so many people, she would believe it, because that was all she had to go on. But she knew what life outside was really like and this she could compare with conditions in China—secretly, I mean, within herself, and with me and her sister. She is like most women. She likes nice dresses, likes to have her hair styled every so often. But on the other hand, she came from the Chinese countryside and doesn't mind hard work.

Kai-yen always expressed the desire to return to Hong Kong. Ever since we got married, she had been in the process of relearning about all those things that she had been taught by the Communists. One thing, of course, that she was concerned about, a thing I was concerned about, too, was the crime rate in the United States, which the Chinese newspapers always made a point of to show how decadent, how corrupt the American society is. And she was concerned about the racial problem in America. She felt sorry for the Negro people and she always asked me why they are beaten up and thrown into jail.

In China all Negroes are discriminated against, the Negroes in our group and also the Africans in Peking University. To the day I left no African had graduated from a Chinese university. Most of them left in disgust after a few years because of discrimination. This discrimination against black people in particular is a social thing; it is not something that has been advocated by the Party. It's just that the people are ignorant, and it has always been traditional among Chinese peasants that the darker one's skin, the more lowly his birth. It is very common among Chinese for people with light skin to look down on those with darker skin from the southern part of China. It is something that all Africans ran into there.

I remember the first African who came to Peking University in about 1959 or '60. Everybody knew him as "Banda," and he was really a rascal. He played up being an African. He went around and borrowed money from the other foreign students and the Chinese. He would go into a hotel and order a huge meal and just sign the name of the university's foreign student department. One time he borrowed 30 *yuan* from a Hungarian student and when the Hungarian pressed him for it, Banda brought him a roll of bills. When he counted it after Banda left, he found just half of what he was owed. That was the way Banda operated. He went around loudly asking girls if they would sleep with him. Of course, they all complained to the Foreign Students Office, but they would say, "Well, he's from Africa and maybe that is his custom." Or, "You should try to unite with him against imperialism."

Banda didn't have much luck with the girls in the school so one night he found a prostitute in town and brought her back in a taxi. When he got near the main gate, he told the girl to get down in the car. Of course, the driver heard this and he stopped at the gate house and told the guard there was a girl lying in the back of his taxi. The gatekeeper opened the door and yanked her out. Banda was furious; he jumped out, knocked the man down. There were three or four Chinese around, and they all came rushing out and piled on Banda. He was strong and he knocked the hell out of the whole lot and fled across the campus with the girl and got into his room.

Banda was a little drunk to start with anyhow and then he got to drinking some more. The gatekeeper alerted the school police and they came around knocking on Banda's door and told him the girl had to go. He shouted back that she was going to stay with him all night. He locked the door and wouldn't let anyone in. Finally, about one o'clock Banda had to go to the latrine and he opened the door and as soon as he was around the corner, they rushed in and grabbed the girl. She screamed, and Banda came dashing back and they had another big fight in the hall. They overpowered him and dragged him off to the school police station with the girl.

At the station he got into another fight and got away and ran. He went back to his room and drank some more and at about three o'clock he came hunting for the Party Secretary. He got hold of two officials and beat them up. This went on until the police came and arrested him and took him away.

Immediately, the other Africans got together and demanded that the Chinese release Banda. They said he was an African and they were discriminating against Africans. They let him out after a few days but ordered him to leave the country as soon as he could. He strutted all over the campus for a while, saying the Chinese can't touch me, and then he left. Went back to Africa.

Whites are discriminated against, too. The Chinese discriminate against all foreigners. Their dislike of foreigners goes way back. I suppose it is connected with the clan type of life the Chinese have always led. A stranger in the village was always a stranger. He would be treated well enough, but he would be an object of suspicion and would be dealt with very cautiously. And they have this same feeling toward anyone who is not Chinese. The Chinese feel their civilization is much older and much better. Foreigners are just clumsy, crude, hairy, smelly.

The Chinese don't know how much damage they have done themselves treating foreigners with suspicion, and treating with isolation foreign students who later became diplomats. I had many friends in the embassies in Peking; many of them had been students with me when they were younger and then had returned to Peking as diplomats, rising to higher and higher positions as the years passed. Among my fellow students were those who became attachés and clerks in the embassies of the United Arab Republic, Indonesia, Bulgaria; a chargé d'affaires in the Norwegian embassy; second secretaries in the Yugoslav and Polish embassies.

One friend of mine was the second secretary in the Russian embassy; I knew him as "Royal." He was a dynamic, inquisitive young man with a pretty wife. He had a short crew cut and dressed like an American. He continually wanted to know how the Chinese thought. He asked: Was there any way for Russia and China to have a meeting of minds? The longer he stayed in the embassy, the more frustrated he became. When an incident occurred between the two countries, the Chinese would take his Chinese language instructor away. He would ask me repeatedly how he could become friends with the Chinese. They never gave him the chance.

In the early years, until 1957 I'd say, I was not terribly aware of this antiforeign feeling—even against Americans. The feeling then among Chinese was that if you were in China, you were good, you were working with the Chinese. They always tend to look at everything very simply, as either black or white. But after the Sino-Soviet split, the Party relaxed its controls on the traditional antiforeign feeling and later even gave impetus to bringing this prejudice back.

One of the first things I was aware of as soon as I returned to America was that I wasn't being stared at all the time; everywhere a foreigner goes in China, he is constantly looked at, watched, stared at. You are under constant watch. And it still bothers you even after you've been there for years.

After a while, a foreigner has the growing suspicion that his mail is being tampered with. You find a tear or extra glue on the envelope. And it takes longer for a letter to reach you from the Peking post office than it took from New York to Peking. Old foreigners know it is being tampered with; young arrivals don't want to believe it. People like Sydney Rittenberg and Sidney Shapiro were sure the Americans were doing it; I was sure the Chinese were. Once it took ten days for me to get a letter from the British Embassy asking me to come over before a diplomat left for a two-month trip. By the time the letter got through to me, he had gone. I urged the British to protest, but I found the British the most cautious embassy in Peking.

Now, of course, Americans are under the greatest suspicion. Nothing good is ever said about America. The Chinese policy is to degrade, to slander, to do anything that would downgrade the Americans or America. Americans share this position with the Russians.

China's prime objective is to kick America out of Asia, to get her out one way or another, and they aren't going to talk about anything else until the United States gets out.

In American foreign policy I consider myself a conservative. I think we should continue the policy of containment of China; there is no chance of negotiating with them and still expecting to stay in Asia. Negotiations with the Chinese don't mean anything: they are not going to compromise. They don't have any conception of equality; they aren't capable of thinking like that. They think of dominance or suppression.

I believe the white man still has a place in Asia, but he won't have it for long. The Chinese policy is to push him out of Asia. They may allow the white man to live there, but he won't have any power. China considers Asia her sphere, and her policy is directed at that completely throughout Asia, with the exception of India. That means Southeast Asia, eventually Japan and Indonesia are to be taken over by communism. The Chinese realize that practically their only antagonist toward reaching this goal is the United States. Once they get rid of the United States in Asia, it's just a matter of walking in. The British certainly can't hold them and there's not much the Russians can do either. Australia is too small. The U.S. is the number one Chinese enemy; that's why they have attacked the U.S. for all these years.

When I left China, I was convinced that the feeling in Peking was that there must be a war with the United States. They felt they have to have a war with the U.S. and they want one now—preferably on their own terms. The Chinese leadership believes the only way to get the U.S. out of Asia is to have a long war with the Americans, preferably a land war. They envision something like the Japanese war—a war to get us involved on land, something that will take years and years and years, and drag on and on and on. This is a major point with them. Time means nothing. They would draw us in and figure after ten years the American people will get tired of it and the people will make the government withdraw from Asia. The Chinese feel it would be a long thing, but in the end U.S. power will be completely eliminated from Asia. And that's what the Chinese want.

In the early years I felt the U.S. should withdraw from Taiwan and eventually from Asia. Get out. That was, I believed, the only way to have peace with China. But over the years that has changed; now I believe the opposite.

I am convinced that there are only two courses open to the United States if we want to come to terms with China: one is to get out—lock, stock, and barrel—from Asia. Taiwan, Southeast Asia and eventually Japan, too. The Chinese now feel that we have to get out completely. The only other course is to stay in Asia and maintain a policy of containment, though I prefer to call it something else so it won't prick so hard. Under this policy, we would let it be known that we are going to maintain our presence even at the cost of nuclear war. I'm convinced that's the only thing that will keep the Chinese from constantly expanding. Very definitely, fear that the U.S. would bomb China stopped her from going into South Vietnam in force in 1965.

I have changed my views through my experiences and what I learned from my Chinese friends. During my years in China, I gained some understanding of Chinese psychology and their methods of dealing with things. And I learned something of Chinese society and of Chinese Communism, which is more Chinese than communist. I have been influenced by my Chinese friends, especially those in rather high positions, who throughout the years have confided in me. Now I do not believe that conciliation will work.

When I left, the focal point was Vietnam. A year before that, the feeling in Peking was that the United States would withdraw from Vietnam without a fight. The Chinese really thought the demonstrations in the United States would force the government to give up. That's why Chinese policy was to help stir up demonstrations in America and Britain and why they organized the foreigners in Peking to help send out propaganda. They tried to get a broad united front among foreigners in China. I was called in, but I didn't get involved because I was already planning to leave. The Chinese also got Westerners to come and would sneak them into North Vietnam. A number of Americans came.

The Chinese tried to make it look as if there was going to be a third world war, and on the side helped to stir up as much opposition as possible inside America and Britain. If America had withdrawn from Vietnam, in a matter of months, the Vietcong would have taken over, and, of course, the Vietcong are under Chinese influence: They are backed by the Chinese. I knew this from Vietnamese whom I had known at Peking University. Several of them were good friends. They thought and spoke like Chinese, but they had a feeling of nationalism, a pride in their small country.

On the contrary, the Americans came into Vietnam in force. This was something the Chinese had not expected. They were set back. And when the United States started bombing North Vietnam, Chinese I knew felt that the Americans had gone too far. The Chinese propaganda had been that if the Americans did anything to a socialist country, it was going to mean a world war. At that point, I too thought the Chinese would go in. There was high excitement in Peking. The Chinese thought the Chinese Army would now go into North Vietnam, and then Peking would be bombed, too.

Right after that, the Chinese leaders felt that President

Johnson had made it clear that if they did come into the war, the Americans would bomb mainland China, her industries, her atomic installations. From that time, all the excitement died away. China did not go in, and her leaders did lose face among their own people. If they thought they could have gotten away with a land war alone in Vietnam, I am sure they would have gone in. But after that crisis, I felt it would take a major land invasion of North Vietnam by the U.S. before the Chinese would move into Vietnam.

The Vietnamese thing is a little special, because the Chinese have limitations there. They couldn't match what the Americans could put into Vietnam; the only people who could were the Russians, but they were being prevented from doing so by the Chinese, as much as possible. And there were differences between the Chinese and the North Vietnamese. The Chinese wanted to send in support troops, but the North Vietnamese wouldn't let them. On at least two occasions, the Chinese made requests to send in troops but the North Vietnamese refused it. The Vietnamese have a deadly fear of the Chinese. Ho Chi Minh told Alan Winnington, who came to visit me after his trip to Hanoi, that the North Vietnamese would never let the Chinese in, because if they did, they would never get them out again. Winnington said North Vietnam was then ready to settle for an independent and neutral South Vietnam, but the Chinese were not ready to settle for that. Vietnam then considered the 17th Parallel a reality; the Chinese didn't. (Winnington also told me that the North Vietnamese claimed their pilots didn't perform well because they blacked out. They thought it was a matter of body chemistry and a lack of training.)

Once the Chinese felt the U.S. had made it clear that she would bomb mainland China, they eased up their propaganda and decided to be much more cautious in Vietnam. Those are the only things they fear—the U.S. Air Force and nuclear weapons. If we made it clear that we were going to use nuclear weapons, the Chinese wouldn't come into Vietnam; but if they did come in, the U.S. should not hesitate to destroy their communications and transportation and centers like Peking and Shanghai. I know these people were friends of mine, but this is a question of life and death. If you are going to get involved in war, fight the war and win it. If you can't win it, then don't get involved, or get out. I can't believe in halfway measures in war, like in Korea.

Just before I left, I thought about the possibility of war between the United States and China. I thought quite a bit about what would happen to me and my wife and child if we got caught there when war started between the U.S. and China. If we didn't get killed in a bombing raid, I'd have been locked up in a camp. This thought helped me make my decision to leave China.

The basic thing is that the Chinese will do anything to achieve an end. Their only principle is that the end must be reached. How it is reached doesn't matter.

Today I feel this way: Chinese Communism is something that is intolerable for a Westerner. To the Oriental, it seems more tolerable; he can live with it. Of course, in China the Party not only controls the government, it owns it. It is their government. There is only one party and they aren't going to tolerate any other parties. But once the people of a communist country accept that fact, which most of them do, they forget about it. It is not thought of at all. They can't even imagine anything else. Of course, freedom of knowledge, freedom of the press, freedom to vote are all assets of a free society, which you don't have there. But few people there understand such privileges.

The police state and this hideous system of everyone spying on everyone else and reporting on them make the communist system intolerable for most foreigners who live there. I admire the security that the system provides for an individual, but I'd like to see a planned society without the police state aspect of it. That's what I think would be ideal.

What would happen to people who don't conform, I don't know. I've never thought much along these lines.

Of course, the security of their system also has its drawbacks. In China, people are leisurely. No one cares what time it is; time doesn't really matter. You get there when you get there. Most people work only because they have to make a living. They have no personal purpose of their own. They don't care if a job gets done, or when it gets done. The only thing that keeps them going is criticism. If they don't accomplish what they're told to accomplish in a certain time, they get bashed. They don't have the same personal drive we do.

Another aspect of the system that foreigners find intolerable is the suppression of religion. Communists don't believe in life after death. To them, the only difference between man and an animal is the development of man's brain. There is no sense of soul, and his only biological duty is the procreation of the race.

On paper, Chinese Protestants and Catholics, for example, are supposed to have the right to go to church. But that's only on paper. In reality, the Party doesn't believe in any church or religion. Their policy is to eliminate it entirely, decimate the number of people attending church, little by little; not allow the children to begin attending church. The whole thing is carried out not through law but by social pressure. It is done through the organization or street committee to which everyone in China belongs and over which the Party has control. That's what has happened over the years, until now only a few old Chinese still attend church. The whole thing is drying up; very, very few people go to church. It will only be a matter of years before there is no church or any religious group there at all.

I know plenty of Chinese who today would welcome a change in government, but who would never make a move to make that change. They expressed this to me very openly. I was trusted by them, and because I wouldn't report them,

I was less trusted by the official Chinese. These people I know object to the scarcity of things and the rationing. They object to China's nuclear development policy; they realize that the more the government spends on bombs, the less they will have to eat and wear and use. Some of them dislike the Chinese attitude of being so terribly anti-America. A number of these people had contacts with Americans before the Communists took over; they are very friendly toward America. But they have to be cautious and when there is a demonstration, they grab their banner and go out and wave it just as hard as anyone else and they shout as hard as anyone else. But what's really in their hearts is very hard to say.

I got a clue one evening in January 1965 when I was talking with my friend who worked for Chou En-lai and he told me that Mao was so angry he couldn't sleep. On the back of the magazine *Chinese Youth* had been published a picture that had antisocialist symbols hidden in it. There was Mao lying dead and Lenin stretched out on his back. In the grass were hidden characters: "Long live Chiang Kai-shek." A couple of days later I told Charles Taylor of the Toronto *Globe and Mail* to look up this magazine. Most of the copies had been picked up, but he finally found one in an embassy and I showed him the symbols. He wrote the story and it made a stir around the world.

I came back from China convinced that if the people in the communist countries show the countries around them and the rest of the world that their system can provide everything and give security to everyone—that no one under their system will starve or be without a place to live and they can share in a clean and moral society, all those things—they will appeal to people and cause more and more people to believe in their system. I don't want the Communists to take over the underdeveloped world, but once people start believing in something, they are going to start working toward that ideal. If it doesn't end in a bloody revolution, it could end in a peaceful transformation. Their internal problems are the only thing that's holding the Chinese Communists back now from taking over, converting, much of the rest of Asia.

When it comes to a choice between these two systems, I don't get the feeling that one hundred percent of the American people would choose liberty over the other. Since I've been back, I've seen a number of things that have shook me up a bit, too. I read the stories in the Chinese papers about poverty here, and I ignored them and took them for pure propaganda. I thought that in a society that has a budget of a hundred billion dollars a year, two cars per family, it just couldn't be possible. But I have seen shocking cases of crime and poverty since I'm back. I have seen rich people get off with suspended sentences and blind people begging on the streets of New York. These things give me the feeling that not everyone here would be one hundred percent American if you gave them the choice between a free capitalist society or a controlled, well-to-do communist country. I know my choice; my experience in China has taught me that. I've come back to compete with everyone else in a free society. But how many people here in America really understand their freedoms?

INDEX

Abaye, Abdula, 106
Adams, Clarence, 14, 76, 91, 116,
    124, 143, 145
Adams, Howard, 14, 122, 123, 143,
    145
Alley, Rewi, 148
Andrews, Mrs. Dorothy (aunt), 15-
    16
Andrews, Joe (uncle), 21
Anti-Rightist Movement, 99-100
Anti-sparrow campaign, 103-4
Antung (China), 73
Arthur, William B., 16
Atomic weapons, *see* Nuclear weap-
    ons

"Baby-sitters," 116-18
Banana Camp, 70
Banda, 169-70
Bandung Conference, 12
Batchelor, Claude, 65, 67, 69, 70
Belhomme, Albert C., 91, 143, 145
Bell, Otto Grayson, 90
Black market of prisoners with Ko-
    reans, 44-45, 52
Borodin, Michael, 12
"Braincoating," 81
Brainwashing
    nature of, 8
    Secretary of Defense's committee
        on, 9-10
    Wills' description of, 18-19, 51-
        59, 65-67, 76-77
    See also Self-criticism
British Marine who defected, *see*
    Condron, Andrew
British POW's, 42, 51
Burchett, Wilfred, 70

Camp One, 47-62
    bombing of, 50
    clothes at, 49
    indoctrination at, 51-59
    marijuana at, 50

Negroes moved from, 51
night blindness at, 49
punishment at, 52-53
quarters at, 48, 51
recreation at, 51
sex at, 49-50
writing home from, 49
Camp 5, 63-67
Canton (China), 164
Chandler, Betty (Betty Chan), 89
Chang, Commander, 65, 67, 68
Chang, Dora, 136
Chase, Alfred, 22-23
Ch'en Yi, 78
China
    Americans visiting, 149
    anti-Communist feeling in, 177-
        78
    Anti-Rightist movement in, 99-
        100
    anti-sparrow campaign in, 103-4
    aristocratic families in rule of,
        144
    dancing in, 84, 107, 116
    economics of, 12-13
        anti-landlord campaign, 109,
            161
        communes, 101, 104, 160-62
        food shortage, 104-5, 124
        factories, 159-60, 162
        food shortage, 104-5, 124
        Great Leap Forward, 12, 95,
            100-1
        private enterprise taken over,
            87
        steel production, 101
    foreigners in
        antiforeign feeling, 121-22,
            170-72
        Chinese girls and, 106-7, 139-
            40
        close watch of, 116-18, 139,
            171
        elite English-speaking group,
            147-51

Negroes, 168-70
police and, 139-42
students, 93, 95-96, 105, 121
travel permits, 139
group social control in, 68
hospitals in, 152-54
Hundred Flowers Movement in,
97-99
intellectuals' distaste of hard labor, 101-2
lack of personal drive in, 177
mobilization of people in, 131-34
anti-sparrow campaign, 103-4
steel production, 101
noise in, 104
nuclear bombs and, 87-88, 145-
47, 150, 178
police in, 139-42, 158-59, 176-77
population problems in, 162
religion in, 177
Russia and, 11-12
basic difference between Chinese and Russian Commu-
nism, 150-51
Chinese policy to cause war between U.S. and Russia, 146
Chinese praise of Russia, 83-84
Cuban missile crisis, 130
start of dispute, 95-96
Vietnam war, 175
Russian military personnel in, 92
self-criticism in, see Self-criticism
United States and
anti-Americanism, 11, 172, 178
attitudes to Kennedy and Johnson, 137
Chinese policy, 146, 172-76
possible war with U.S., 172-
73, 176
White Russians in, 85-86, 92
Wills in, 10, 71-165
attacks Mao's theory, 150
buys shortwave radio, 90-91
in Chinese film, 130-31
courtship and marriage, 107-
19, 167
disillusionment, 13, 72, 112-15,
119-22, 152-53
as English teacher, 157-58

at Foreign Language Press,
124-29, 135, 145, 155-56
household life, 124-25
indoctrination, 76-77
questioned on nuclear installations, 87-88
self-criticism, 10, 77-81, 84, 91
terms he was addressed by, 155
threatens to leave China, 112,
115
visit to hospital, 152-53
See also Peking
China Pictorial, 124, 163
Chinese army
in control of ex-POW's, 76, 82
discipline of, 43
Chinese Red Cross, 82, 122, 143,
155, 159
Wills' exit from China and, 156,
159, 163-65
Wills' marriage and, 110-16, 119
Chinese Youth, 178
Chou En-lai, 102, 113, 126, 144
forgery of signature of, 131-32
Wills' meeting with, 135
Clubb, O. Edmund, 12
Coe, Frank, 148
Columbia University, 15
Communes, 101, 104, 160-62
Communism, future of, 81
Condron, Andrew (British Marine),
6, 14, 65, 71, 92
Corden, Richard G., 65, 67, 70, 89,
91
Cowart, William A., 73-74, 90
Criticism-and-self-criticism, see Self-
criticism
Cuban missile crisis (1962), 130
Cult of the personality, 13, 95-96

Dancing, 84, 107, 116
Daily Worker, 52, 53
Dairen (China), 92
Death march, 36-47
American bombings, 36, 39, 45-
46
black market with Koreans, 44-45
food on, 35-37, 39-40

Death march (*Continued*)
  punishment of escapees, 43-44
Dickenson, Edward S., 69
Douglas, Rufus E., 75
Dunn, John R., 102-3

Epstein, Israel, 126, 148

Filipino POW's, 42
"54 Days of White Terror, The,"
  134
Food
  at Camp One, 48
  on death march, 35-37, 39-40
  at Peking University, 93-94
Ford Foundation, 15
Foreign Languages Press, 124-29,
  135, 145, 155-56
  diary of Lei Feng at, 127-28
  Letters to the Editors, 128-29
Foreign Languages Press Training
  School, 157-58
Foreigners, *see* China—foreigners
  in
Fort Ann, N.Y., 77
  See also West Fort Ann
Fortuna, Andrew, 91, 92

Germ warfare confessions, 9, 58
Gibson, Nancy, 4, 165
Gilmore, Miss (teacher), 21-22
"Giveupitis," 37
Graves, Sonny, 23
Great Leap Forward, 12, 95, 100-1
Greene, Felix, 142, 153
Greenfield, James L., 3
Griggs, Lewis W., 90

Hakkah minority, 109
Han Suyin, 114
Hansen, James, 3, 4
Harvard University East Asian Re-
  search Center, 2, 15
Hatem, George, 148
Hawkins, Samuel D., 91
Hinton, Joan, 148

Ho Chi Minh, 175
Hodes, William, 84-85
Hodson, Thomas A. H., 4, 165
Homosexuality, 50
Hong Kong
  education in, 110
  Wills arrives at, 1, 3-4, 165
Hu Feng movement, 84
Hu Shih, 84
Hundred Flowers Movement, 97-99
Hungarian revolt, 96-97

Indian Army in neutral zone, 6, 67-
  70

Jail in Peking, 162-63
Johnson, Lyndon B., Chinese attitude to, 137, 174-75

Kaesong, Korea, 68, 71
Kai-yen, *see* Wills, Mrs. Morris R.
Kao Yu-pao, 83
Kennedy, John F.
  assassination of, 135-36
  Chinese attitude to, 136-37
Klein, Donald W., 4
Khrushchev, Nikita, 95
Korean War
  American POW's in
    deaths among, 8
    number captured, 8
    See also Brainwashing; Camp
      One; Death March; Negroes;
      Returnees to China; Wills,
      Morris R.—as prisoner of
      Chinese
  China's entry into, 11
  killing of Chinese prisoners in,
    27-28
  Russians in, 46
  Wills in, 5, 25-33
    attitude toward winning the
      war, 54
    wounded, 28-29

Lei Feng, diary of, 127-28, 167
Leztov, Sasha, 95

Lice, 40
Lindbeck, John M. H., 16
Liu Shao-chi, 132
    Mao and, 134
Lohman, Joseph D., in Operation
    Big Switch, 6-7
Look magazine, 2-3, 16
Luo (Wills' "baby-sitter"), 117-18
Lushan (China), 144

MacArthur, Gen. Douglas, 54
Mao Tse-tung, 102, 178
    on atomic war, 150
    birthplace of, 144
    cult of personality and, 96
    Cultural Revolution of, 13, 134
    Hundred Flowers Movement of,
        98
    Liu and, 134
    secret war headquarters of, 146
Marijuana, 50, 66
Marriages of Americans and Chi-
    nese, 111, 122-24
    Wills' marriage, 107-19
Marxism, Wills' lack of knowledge
    of, 55
Ming Tombs, 102-3

Needham, Joseph, 126
Negroes
    in China, 168-70
    in P.O.W. camps, 51, 53
    self-criticism meetings and, 80
Neutral zone, POW's in, 6-7, 67-
    71
Nuclear weapons
    in China, 87-88, 145-47, 178
    Mao's thesis on, 150
    Wills' attitude toward, 54, 175-
        76

Operation Big Switch, 6-7, 67-71
Operation Killer, 27

Passports of Americans who enter
    China, 149
Pate, Arlie H., 122

Peace appeals in Korean War, 57
Peitaiho (China), 132, 138-40
Peking (China)
    airfield in, 157-58
    anti-sparrow campaign in, 103-4
    bakery in, 160
    demonstrations in, 129-30
    factories in, 159-60, 162
    foreign movies in, 125
    Foreign Languages Institute in,
        91
    jail in, 162-63
    People's University in, 82-84, 89-
        91
    public execution in, 86
    recreation in, 84-86
    University of, 92-99, 124
        foreign students at, 93, 95-96,
            105, 121
        Hundred Flowers Movement
            at, 98-100
        steel production at, 101
        sports at, 94
        Wills' marriage and, 111, 116,
            119
        "unofficial" system in, 118-19
Peking Review, 135
Penfound, Mr. (teacher), 21
Ping-Pong, 84, 107
Platt, Nicholas, 4, 165
POW's, *see* Korean War—Ameri-
    can POW's in
Pyongyang, Korea, 71

Red Cross, *see* Chinese Red Cross
Red Guard, 134, 167-68
Returnees from China, 14, 122, 145
    Chinese policy on, 123, 143, 156-
        57
    prosecution of, 7-8, 90
Ridgway, Gen. Matthew B., 16
Rittenberg, Sydney, 148, 171
Rush, Scott L., 91, 143, 145
Russia
    China and, 11-12
        basic difference between Chi-
            nese and Russian Commu-
            nism, 150-51

Russia, China and (Continued)
  Chinese policy to cause war between U.S. and Russia, 146
  Chinese praise of Russia, 83-84
  Cuban missile crisis, 130
  start of dispute, 95-96
  Vietnam war, 175
  purges of 1930's in, 8
Russians
  in China, 92
  White Russians, 85-86, 92
  in Korean War, 46

Schuman, Julian, 148
Secretary of Defense's Advisory Committee on Prisoners of War, 9-10
Self-criticism, 10, 150-51
  autobiographies in, 53, 78, 84
  described, 77-81
  at People's University, 84, 91
  Wills's first experience with, 65
Sex
  among P.O.W.'s, 49-50
  in China, 84-86, 106-7
Shanghai (China), 84
Shanghai News, 51, 52
Shapiro, Michael, 148, 151
Shapiro, Sidney, 130-31, 138, 148-50, 157, 171
Shortwave radios, 90-91
Sinuiju, Korea, 46
Skinner, Lowell, 123-24, 143, 145
Snow, Edgar, 142, 153
Socialist Education Movement, Ssu Ching phase of, 132-134
Soong Ching-ling, 114
Soviet Union, see Russia
Spanish Civil War, 148
Ssu Ching Movement, 132-34
Stevenson, Michael, 3
Strong, Anna Louise, 148
Suicides in China, 100, 109
Sullivan, LaRance, 67, 75, 89, 91
Sun, Robert, 3

Taiyüan (China), 73-81, 91, 144
Tangshan (China), 88-89

Tannenbaum, Gerald, 131, 148
Taylor, Charles, 15, 178
Tenneson, Richard R., 15, 64, 122
Tien, Commander, 65, 66, 71, 73-74
Tientsin (China), 88, 111-13
Time magazine, 97
Tobacco, 38, 43
Tsinan (China), 122-24
Tsingtao (China), 142-43
Tung Hua-yao, 94
Turkish POW's, discipline of, 42

United States
  China and
    anti-Americanism, 11, 172, 178
    attitudes to Kennedy and Johnson, 137
    Chinese policy, 146, 172-76
    possible war with U.S., 172-73, 176
  poverty in, 179

Veneris, James G., 14, 143, 144
Vietnam, 58, 76, 147
  Chinese policy toward, 173-76
  U.S. movement against war in, 148-49, 151
  Wills' statements from China on, 130
Voice of America, 91, 122, 125

Wall posters, in Hundred Flowers Movement, 98-99
Wang Kuang-mei, 132-34
Webb, Harold, 91
West Fort Ann, N.Y., 19
  Wills' return to, 15-16
  See also Fort Ann
White, William C., 92, 116, 143, 144
Wills (brother), 21
Wills (father), 16, 20-21, 23, 25
Wills, Mrs. (mother), 15, 20-21, 61
Wills, Morris R.
  ancestry of, 19

birth of, 19
boyhood of, 5, 19-24
in China, 10, 71-165
  attacks Mao's theory, 150
  buys shortwave radio, 90-91
  in Chinese film, 130-31
  courtship and marriage, 107-19, 167
  disillusionment, 13, 72, 112-15, 119-22, 152-53
  as English teacher, 157-58
  at Foreign Languages Press, 124-29, 135, 145, 155-56
  household life, 124-25
  indoctrination, 76-77
  questioned on nuclear installations, 87-88
  self-criticism, 10, 77-81, 84, 91
  terms he was addressed by, 155
  threatens to leave China, 112, 115
  visit to hospital, 152-53
  See also Peking
joins Army, 24-25
in Korean War, 5, 25-33
  attitude toward winning the war, 54
  wounded, 28-29
leaves China
  arrival at Hong Kong, 1, 3-4, 165
  decision to leave China, 2-3, 155-56
  formalities involved, 156, 158-59

as prisoner of Chinese, 5-7, 33-71
  at Camp 5, 63-67
  captured, 33
  decides to go to China, 59-64
  indoctrination and brainwashing, 5-6, 18-19, 51-59, 65-67
  memories of lima beans, 26
  in Operation Big Switch, 6-7, 67-71
  signing peace appeals, 57
  writing autobiographies, 53
  See also Camp One; Death March
after return to U.S., 15-16
  attitude toward China today, 18, 166-79
Wills, Mrs. Morris R. (Kai-yen) (wife), 104, 124-25, 136
  attitude toward China of, 167-68
  birth of daughter, 153-55
  courtship and marriage of, 107-19, 167
  leaves China, 158, 163-65
  in prison, 112-15
Wilson, Aaron P., 76, 122
Wilson, Charles E., 7-8
Winchell, Jimmy, 16, 23, 25-26
Winnington, Alan, 70, 76, 89, 175
Winnington, Mrs. Alan, 138-39
Wuhan (China), 91, 105

Yaan (China), 146
Yangku, China, *see* Taiyüan
Yi Cheng-hsin, 156

DATE DUE

MAR 1